THAT
INCREDIBLE
CHRISTIAN

From Elaine

D0227591

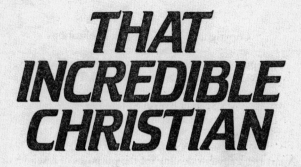

THAT INCREDIBLE CHRISTIAN

A. W. TOZER

OM Publishing
Bromley, Kent

First published in the USA by Christian Publications,
3825 Hartzdale Drive, Camp Hill, PA 17011

Second British edition 1989
Reprinted 1991

Biblical quotations are from the Authorised Version
(Crown copyright)

British Library Cataloguing in Publication Data

Wilson, A. W. (Aiden Wilson), *1897–1963*
   That Incredible Christian.–2nd ed
   I. Title
   248.4

ISBN 1-85078-064-1

OM Publishing is an imprint of Send The Light
(Operation Mobilisation),
PO Box 48, Bromley, Kent, England, BR1 3JH

Production and Printing in England by
Nuprint Ltd, Station Road, Harpenden, Herts AL5 4SE.

Contents

Acknowledgements

Most of the chapters of this book appeared as editorials in *The Alliance Witness*, of which Dr Tozer was editor, during the years 1960–1963. 'The Art of True Worship' appeared originally in *Moody Monthly* (1952) and is included here with their kind permission.

Publisher's Introduction

Someone said that while Dr A. W. Tozer always sought to introduce sinners to their Saviour, he longed to help saints to see the greatness of God and to experience the life of victory and joy through surrender and faith. This theme–recognising God for who He is, giving Him the worship and honour due Him–was particularly dominant in Dr Tozer's late writings.

To know God requires first of all a right relationship to Him. It requires time, and this we must give. It requires also faith and knowledge, and this God gives as we humbly seek Him. And because we cannot know God apart from the illuminating Holy Spirit, we must welcome Him, allowing Him to indwell and possess us.

The reader will find each chapter in this book complete in itself, and one may speak to him more than another. There is, however, progression, and greater profit will come from at least one consecutive reading.

The chapters were selected to instruct the heart that seeks 'to follow on to know the Lord'. Such a life may not be always easy, but at the last it will be all that really matters.

1

That Incredible Christian

The current effort of so many religious leaders to harmonise Christianity with science, philosophy and every natural and reasonable thing is, I believe, the result of failure to understand Christianity and, judging from what I have heard and read, failure to understand science and philosophy as well.

At the heart of the Christian system lies the cross of Christ with its divine paradox. The power of Christianity appears in its antipathy toward, never in its agreement with, the ways of fallen men. The truth of the cross is revealed in its contradictions. The witness of the church is most effective when she declares rather than explains, for the gospel is addressed not to reason but to faith. What can be proved requires no faith to accept. Faith rests upon the character of God, not upon the demonstrations of laboratory or logic.

The cross stands in bold opposition to the natural man. Its philosophy runs contrary to the processes of the unregenerate mind, so that Paul could say bluntly that the preaching of the cross is to them that perish foolishness. To try to find a common ground between the message of the cross and man's fallen reason is to try the impossible, and if persisted in must result in an impaired reason, a meaningless cross and a powerless Christianity.

But let us bring the whole matter down from the uplands of theory and simply observe the true Christian as he puts into practice the teachings of Christ and His apostles. Note the contradictions:

The Christian believes that in Christ he has died, yet he is more alive than before and he fully expects to live for ever. He walks on earth while seated in heaven and though born on earth he finds that after his conversion he is not at home here. Like the night-hawk, which in the air is the essence of grace and beauty but on the ground is awkward and ugly, so the Christian appears at his best in the heavenly places but does not fit well into the ways of the very society into which he was born.

The Christian soon learns that if he would be victorious as a son of heaven among men on earth he must not follow the common pattern of mankind, but rather the contrary. That he may be safe he puts himself in jeopardy; he loses his life to save it and is in danger of losing it if he attempts to preserve it. He goes down to get up. If he refuses to go down he is already down, but when he starts down, he is on his way up.

He is strongest when he is weakest and weakest when he is strong. Though poor he has the power to make others rich, but when he becomes rich his ability to enrich others vanishes. He has most after he has given most away and has least when he possesses most.

He may be and often is highest when he feels lowest and most sinless when he is most conscious of sin. He is wisest when he knows that he knows not and knows least when he has acquired the greatest amount of knowledge. He sometimes does most by doing nothing and goes furthest when standing still. In heaviness he manages to rejoice and keeps his heart glad even in sorrow.

The paradoxical character of the Christian is revealed constantly. For instance, he believes that he is saved now, nevertheless he expects to be saved later and looks forward joyfully to future salvation. He fears God but is not afraid of Him. In God's presence he feels overwhelmed and undone, yet there is nowhere he would rather be than in that presence. He knows that he has been cleansed from his sin, yet he is painfully conscious that in his flesh dwells no good thing.

He loves supremely one whom he has never seen, and though himself poor and lowly he talks familiarly with one who is King of all kings and Lord of all lords, and is aware of no incongruity in so doing. He feels that he is in his own right altogether less than nothing, yet he believes without question that he is the apple of God's eye and that for him the Eternal Son became flesh and died on the cross of shame.

The Christian is a citizen of heaven and to that sacred citizenship he acknowledges first allegiance; yet he may love his earthly country with that intensity of devotion that caused John Knox to pray 'O God, give me Scotland or I die.'

He cheerfully expects before long to enter that bright world above, but he is in no hurry to leave this world and is quite willing to await the summons of his Heavenly Father. And he is unable to understand why the critical unbeliever should condemn him for this; it all seems so natural and right in the circumstances that he sees nothing inconsistent about it.

The cross-carrying Christian, furthermore, is both a confirmed pessimist and an optimist the like of which is to be found nowhere else on earth.

When he looks at the cross he is a pessimist, for he knows that the same judgement that fell on the Lord of glory condemns in that one act all nature and all the world of men. He rejects every human hope out of Christ because he knows that man's noblest effort is only dust building on dust.

Yet he is calmly, restfully optimistic. If the cross condemns the world the resurrection of Christ guarantees the ultimate triumph of good throughout the universe. Through Christ all will be well at last and the Christian waits the consummation. Incredible Christian!

2

Time Cannot Help Us

Sin has done frightful things to us and its effect upon us is all the more deadly because we were born in it and are scarcely aware of what is happening to us.

One thing sin has done is to confuse our values so that we can only with difficulty distinguish a friend from a foe or tell for certain what is and what is not good for us. We walk in a world of shadows where real things appear unreal and things of no consequence are sought after as eagerly as if they were made of the very gold that paves the streets of the City of God.

Our ideas rarely accord with things as they are, but are distorted by a kind of moral astigmatism that throws everything out of focus. Through a multitude of errors our total philosophy is out of line, somewhat as our mathematics would be had we learned the multiplication table wrongly and not been aware of our mistake.

One false concept to which we cling tenaciously is time. We think of it as being a sort of viscid substance flowing onward like a sluggish river, bearing upon its bosom nations and empires and civilisations and men. We visualise this sticky stream as an entity and ourselves as helplessly stuck in it for as long as our earthly lives endure.

Or again, by a simple shift in our thinking we picture

time as a revealer of the shape of things to come, as when we say 'Time will tell'. Or we imagine it a benign physician and comfort ourselves with the thought that 'time is a great healer'. All this is so much a part of us that it would be too much to expect that the habit of referring everything to time could ever be broken. Yet we may guard against the harm that such thinking carries with it.

The most harmful mistake we make concerning time is that it has somehow a mysterious power to perfect human nature. We say of a foolish young man, 'Time will make him wiser,' or we see a new Christian acting like anything but a Christian and hope that time will some day turn him into a saint.

The truth is that time has no more power to sanctify a man than space has. Indeed, time is only a fiction by which we account for change. It is change, not time, that turns fools into wise men and sinners into saints. Or more accurately, it is Christ who does the whole thing by means of the changes He works in the heart.

Saul the persecutor became Paul the servant of God, but time did not make the change. Christ wrought the miracle, the same Christ who once changed water into wine. One spiritual experience followed another in fairly rapid succession until the violent Saul became a gentle, God-enamoured soul ready to lay down his life for the faith he once hated. It should be obvious that time had no part in the making of the man of God.

My purpose in writing this little piece is not to engage in an exercise in semantics but to alert my readers to the injury they may suffer from an unfounded confidence in time. Because a Moses and a Jacob lost the impulsive, headstrong sins of their youth and in their old age became gentle, mellow saints we tend to take it for granted that time wrought the transformation. But it is not so. God, not time, makes saints.

Human nature is not fixed, and for this we should thank God day and night. We are still capable of change.

We can become something other than what we are. By the power of the gospel the covetous man may become generous, the egotist lowly in his own eyes. The thief may learn to steal no more, the blasphemer to fill his mouth with praises unto God. But it is Christ who does it all. Time has nothing to do with it.

Many a lost man is putting off the day of salvation, vaguely hoping that time is on his side, when actually the likelihood of his ever becoming a Christian grows less day by day. And why? Because the changes taking place in him are hardening his will and making it more and more difficult for him to repent.

> Seek ye the Lord while he may be found, call ye upon him while he is near. Let the wicked forsake his way, and the unrighteous man his thoughts: and let him return unto the Lord, and he will have mercy upon him; and to our God, for he will abundantly pardon. (Isa 55:6,7.)

See the change-words in this text: 'Seek...call...forsake...return.' These all denote specific changes the returning sinner must make in himself, acts that he must perform. But this is not enough. 'Have mercy ...pardon'; these are the changes God makes in and for the man. To be saved the man must change and be changed.

To enter the kingdom of God, our Lord explained, a man must be born again (Jn 3:3–7). That is, he must undergo a spiritual change. This accords completely with the preaching of John the Baptist who called upon his hearers to prepare the way of the Lord by bringing forth fruits worthy of repentance, and with the apostle Peter who reminded the early Christians that they had been made partakers of the divine nature and had escaped the corruption the world had suffered by lust.

The initial change, however, is not the only one the redeemed man will know. His whole Christian life will consist of a succession of changes, moving always toward spiritual perfection. To achieve these changes the Holy Spirit uses various means, probably the most effective being the writings of the New Testament.

Time can help us only if we know that it cannot help us at all. It is change we need, and only God can change us from worse to better.

3

What It Means to Accept Christ

A few things, fortunately only a few, are matters of life and death, such as a compass for a sea voyage or a guide for a journey across the desert. To ignore these vital things is not to gamble or take a chance; it is to commit suicide. Here it is either be right or be dead.

Our relation to Christ is such a matter of life or death, and on a much higher plane. The Bible-instructed man knows that Jesus Christ came into the world to save sinners and that men are saved by Christ alone altogether apart from any works of merit.

That much is true and is known, but obviously the death and resurrection of Christ do not automatically save everyone. How does the individual man come into saving relation to Christ? That some do we know, but that others do not is evident. How is the gulf bridged between redemption objectively provided and salvation subjectively received? How does that which Christ did for me become operative within me? To the question 'What must I do to be saved?' we must learn the correct answer. To fail here is not to gamble with our souls; it is to guarantee eternal banishment from the face of God. Here we must be right or be finally lost.

To this anxious question evangelical Christians provide three answers, 'Believe on the Lord Jesus Christ,'

'Receive Christ as your personal Saviour,' and 'Accept Christ.' Two of the answers are drawn almost verbatim from the Scriptures (Acts 16:31, Jn 1:12), while the third is a kind of paraphrase meant to sum up the other two. They are therefore not three but one.

Being spiritually lazy we naturally tend to gravitate toward the easiest way of settling our religious questions for ourselves and others; hence the formula 'Accept Christ' has become a panacea of universal application, and I believe it has been fatal to many. Though undoubtedly an occasional serious-minded penitent may find in it all the instruction he needs to bring him into living contact with Christ, I fear that too many seekers use it as a short cut to the Promised Land, only to find that it has led them instead to 'a land of darkness, as darkness itself; and of the shadow of death, without any order, and where the light is as darkness'.

The trouble is that the whole 'Accept Christ' attitude is likely to be wrong. It shows Christ applying to us rather than us to Him. It makes Him stand hat-in-hand awaiting our verdict on Him, instead of our kneeling with troubled hearts awaiting His verdict on us. It may even permit us to accept Christ by an impulse of mind or emotions, painlessly, at no loss to our ego and no inconvenience to our usual way of life.

For this ineffectual manner of dealing with a vital matter we might imagine some parallels; as if, for instance, Israel in Egypt had 'accepted' the blood of the Passover but continued to live in bondage, or the prodigal son had 'accepted' his father's forgiveness and stayed on among the swine in the far country. Is it not plain that if accepting Christ is to mean anything there must be moral action that accords with it?

Allowing the expression 'Accept Christ' to stand as an honest effort to say in short what could not be so well said any other way, let us see what we mean or should mean when we use it.

To accept Christ is to form an attachment to the

person of our Lord Jesus altogether unique in human experience. The attachment is intellectual, volitional and emotional. The believer is intellectually convinced that Jesus is both Lord and Christ; he has set his will to follow Him at any cost and soon his heart is enjoying the exquisite sweetness of His fellowship.

This attachment is all-inclusive in that it joyfully accepts Christ for all that He is. There is no craven division of offices whereby we may acknowledge His Saviourhood today and withhold decision on His lordship till tomorrow. The true believer owns Christ as his all in all without reservation. He also includes all of himself, leaving no part of his being unaffected by the revolutionary transaction.

Further, his attachment to Christ is all-exclusive. The Lord becomes to him not one of several rival interests, but the one exclusive attraction for ever. He orbits around Christ as the earth around the sun, held in thrall by the magnetism of His love, drawing all his life and light and warmth from Him. In this happy state he is given other interests, it is true, but these are all determined by his relation to his Lord.

That we accept Christ in this all-inclusive, all-exclusive way is a divine imperative. Here faith makes its leap into God through the person and work of Christ, but it never divides the work from the person. It never tries to believe on the blood apart from Christ Himself, or the cross or the 'finished work'. It believes on the Lord Jesus Christ, the whole Christ without modification or reservation, and thus it receives and enjoys all that He did in His work of redemption, all that He is now doing in heaven for His own and all that He does in and through them.

To accept Christ is to know the meaning of the words 'as he is, so are we in this world' (1 Jn 4:17). We accept His friends as our friends, His enemies as our enemies, His ways as our ways, His rejection as our rejection, His cross as our cross, His life as our life and His future as our future.

If this is what we mean when we advise the seeker to accept Christ we had better explain it to him. He may get into deep spiritual trouble unless we do.

4

How Important Is Creed?

Among certain Christians it has become quite the fashion to cry down creed and cry up experience as the only true test of Christianity. The expression 'Not creed, but Christ' (taken, I believe, from a poem by John Oxenham) has been widely accepted as the very voice of truth and given a place alongside the writings of prophets and apostles.

When I first heard the words they sounded good. One got from them the idea that the advocates of the no-creed creed had found a precious secret that the rest of us had missed; that they had managed to cut right through the verbiage of historic Christianity and come direct to Christ without bothering about doctrine. And the words appeared to honour our Lord more perfectly by focusing attention upon Him alone and not upon mere words. But is this true? I think not.

In this no-creed creed there are indeed a few grains of real truth, but not as many as the no-creed advocates imagine. And those few are buried beneath a mighty pile of chaff, something that the no-creed people cannot at all imagine.

Now I have a lot of sympathy for the no-creed creedalists for I realise that they are protesting the substitution of a dead creed for a living Christ; and in this I join them whole-heartedly. But this antithesis need not exist; there is no reason for our creeds being dead just as there is no reason for our faith being dead. James tells us that there is such a thing as dead faith, but we do not reject all faith for that reason.

Now the truth is that creed is implicit in every thought, word or act of the Christian life. It is altogether impossible to come to Christ without knowing at least something about Him; and what we know about Him is what we believe about Him; and what we believe about Him is our Christian creed. Otherwise stated, since our creed is what we believe, it is impossible to believe on Christ and have no creed.

Preaching Christ is generally, and correctly, held to be the purest, noblest ministry in which any man can engage; but preaching Christ includes a great deal more than talking about Christ in superlatives. It means more than giving vent to the religious love the speaker feels for the person of Christ. Glowing love for Christ will give fragrance and warmth to any sermon, but it is still not enough. Love must be intelligent and informed if it is to have any permanent meaning. The effective sermon must have intellectual content, and wherever there is intellect there is creed. It cannot be otherwise.

This is not to plead for the use of the historic creeds in our Christian gatherings. I realise that it is entirely possible to recite the Apostles' Creed every Sunday for a lifetime with no profit to the soul. The Nicene Creed may be said or sung in every service without benefiting anyone. The standard creeds are a summary of what the Christian professes to believe, and they are excellent as far as they go yet they may be learned by rote and repeated without conviction and so be altogether stale and unprofitable.

While we may worship (and thousands of Christians do) without the use of any formal creed, it is impossible to worship acceptably without some knowledge of the one we seek to worship. And that knowledge is our creed whether it is ever formalised or not. It is not enough to say that we may have a mystical or numinous experience of God without any doctrinal knowledge and that is sufficient. No, it is not sufficient. We must worship in truth as well as in spirit; and truth can be stated and when it is stated it becomes creed.

The effort to be practising Christians without knowing what Christianity is about must always fail. The true Christian should be, indeed must be, a theologian. He must know at least something of the wealth of truth revealed in the Holy Scriptures. And he must know it with sufficient clarity to state it and defend his statement. And what can be stated and defended is a creed.

Because the heart of the Christian life is admittedly faith in a person, Jesus Christ the Lord, it has been relatively easy for some to press this truth out of all proportion and teach that faith in the person of Christ is all that matters. Who Jesus is matters not, who His Father was, whether Jesus is God or man or both, whether or not He accepted the superstitions and errors of His time as true, whether He actually rose again after His passion or was only thought to have done so by His devoted followers–these things are not important, say the no-creed advocates. What is vital is that we believe on Him and try to follow His teachings.

What is overlooked here is that the conflict of Christ with the Pharisees was over the question of *who He was*. His claim to be God stirred the Pharisees to fury. He could have cooled the fire of their anger by backing away from His claim to equality with God, but He refused to do it. And He further taught that faith in Him embraced a belief that He is very God, and that apart from this there could be no salvation for anyone. 'He said unto them, Ye are from beneath; I am from above: ye are of this world; I am not of this world. I said therefore unto you, that ye shall die in your sins: for if ye believe not that I am he, ye shall die in your sins' (Jn 8:23,24).

To believe on Christ savingly means to believe the right things about Christ. There is no escaping this.

5

The Inadequacy of 'Instant Christianity'

It is hardly a matter of wonder that the country that gave the world instant tea and instant coffee should be the one to give it instant Christianity. If these two beverages were not actually invented in the United States it was certainly here that they received the advertising impetus that has made them known to most of the civilised world. And it cannot be denied that it was American Fundamentalism that brought instant Christianity to the gospel churches.

Ignoring for the moment Romanism, and Liberalism in its various disguises, and focusing our attention upon the great body of evangelical believers, we see at once how deeply the religion of Christ has suffered in the house of its friends. The American genius for getting things done quickly and easily with little concern for quality or permanence has bred a virus that has infected the whole evangelical church in the United States and, through our literature, our evangelists and our missionaries, has spread all over the world.

Instant Christianity came in with the machine age. Men invented machines for two purposes. They wanted to get important work done more quickly and easily than they could do it by hand, and they wanted to get the work over with so they could give their time to pursuits more to their liking, such as loafing or enjoying the pleasures of the world. Instant Christianity now serves the same purposes in religion. It disposes of the past, guarantees the future and sets the Christian free to follow the more refined lusts of the flesh in all good conscience and with a minimum of restraint.

By 'instant Christianity' I mean the kind found almost everywhere in gospel circles and which is born of the notion that we may discharge our total obligation to our own souls by one act of faith, or at most by two, and be relieved thereafter of all anxiety about our spiritual condition. We are saints by calling, our teachers keep telling us, and we are permitted to infer from this that there is no reason to seek to be saints by character. An automatic, once-for-all quality is present here that is completely out of mode with the faith of the New Testament.

In this error, as in most others, there lies a certain amount of truth imperfectly understood. It is true that conversion to Christ may be and often is sudden. Where the burden of sin has been heavy the sense of forgiveness is usually clear and joyful. The delight experienced in forgiveness is equal to the degree of moral repugnance felt in repentance. The true Christian has met God. He knows he has eternal life and he is likely to know where and when he received it. And those also who have been filled with the Holy Spirit subsequent to their regeneration have a clear-cut experience of being filled. The Spirit is self-announcing, and the renewed heart has no difficulty identifying His presence as He floods in over the soul.

But the trouble is that we tend to put our trust in our experiences and as a consequence misread the entire New Testament. We are constantly being exhorted to make the decision, to settle the matter now, to get the whole thing taken care of at once—and those who exhort us are right in doing so. There are decisions that can be and should be made once and for all. There are personal matters that can be settled instantaneously by a determined act of the will in response to Bible-grounded faith. No one would want to deny this; certainly not I.

The question before us is, Just how much can be accomplished in that one act of faith? How much yet remains to be done and how far can a single decision take us?

Instant Christianity tends to make the faith act terminal and so smothers the desire for spiritual advance. It fails to understand the true nature of the Christian life, which is not static but dynamic and expanding. It overlooks the fact that a new Christian is a living organism as certainly as a new baby is, and must have nourishment and exercise to assure normal growth. It does not consider that the act of faith in Christ sets up a personal relationship between two intelligent moral beings, God and the reconciled man, and no single encounter between God and a creature made in His image could ever be sufficient to establish an intimate friendship between them.

By trying to pack all of salvation into one experience, or two, the advocates of instant Christianity flaunt the law of development which runs through all nature. They ignore the sanctifying effects of suffering, cross-carrying and practical obedience. They pass by the need for spiritual training, the necessity of forming right religious habits and the need to wrestle against the world, the devil and the flesh.

Undue preoccupation with the initial act of believing has created in some a psychology of contentment, or at least of non-expectation. To many it has imparted a mood of disappointment with the Christian faith. God seems too far away, the world is too near, and the flesh too powerful to resist. Others are glad to accept the assurance of automatic blessedness. It relieves them of the need to watch and fight and pray, and sets them free to enjoy this world while waiting for the next.

Instant Christianity is twentieth century orthodoxy. I

wonder whether the man who wrote Philippians 3:7–16
would recognise it as the faith for which he finally died. I
am afraid he would not.

6

Faith's Foundation Is God

If our faith is to have a firm foundation we must be convinced beyond any possible doubt that God is altogether worthy of our trust. This conviction must be more than a tenet of our creed to which we give nominal assent. It must penetrate the profoundest depths of our spirits; it must get through all outward forms to the eternal substance of which our beings are composed, that sacred stuff which was once made in the image of God.

As long as we question the wisdom of any of God's ways our faith is still tentative and uncertain. While we are able to understand, we are not quite believing. Faith enters when there is no supporting evidence to corroborate God's word of promise and we must put our confidence blindly in the character of the one who made the promise.

Faith that asked no proof was manifested by our Lord when He was enduring His ordeal of agony on the cross. Though rejected and forsaken, and in His great pain and weakness tempted to wonder how it could be thus with Him, His faith found its rest in the holiness of God: 'But thou art holy, O thou that inhabitest the praises of Israel.' Though the whole world shouted against God and every testimony of the senses was against His goodness and love, Christ knew God was holy and could do no wrong, so He would bear the agony until His Father released Him. Here was faith in its most perfect expression. The faith that made the sun stand still or brought down fire from heaven was elementary compared with this.

Remember that faith is not a noble quality found only in superior men. It is not a virtue attainable by a limited few. It is not the ability to persuade ourselves that black is white or that something we desire will come to pass if we only wish hard enough. Faith is simply the bringing of our minds into accord with the truth. It is adjusting our expectations to the promises of God in complete assurance that the God of the whole earth cannot lie.

A man looks at a mountain and affirms, 'That is a mountain.' There is no particular virtue in the affirmation. It is simply accepting the fact that stands before him and bringing his belief into accord with the fact. The man does not create the mountain by believing, nor could he annihilate it by denying. And so with the truth of God. The believing man accepts a promise of God as a fact as solid as a mountain and vastly more enduring. His faith changes nothing except his own personal relation to the word of promise. God's Word is true whether we believe it or not. Human unbelief cannot alter the character of God.

Faith is subjective, but it is sound only when it corresponds with objective reality. The man's faith in the mountain is valid only because the mountain is there; otherwise it would be mere imagination and would need to be sharply corrected to rescue the man from harmful delusion. So God is what He is in Himself. He does not become what we believe. 'I AM THAT I AM' (Ex 3:14). We are on safe ground only when we know what kind of God He is and adjust our entire being to the holy concept.

Since true faith rests upon what God is, it is of utmost importance that, to the limit of our comprehension, we know what He is. 'They that know thy name will put their trust in thee.' The name of God is the verbal expression of His character, and confidence always rises or falls with known character. What the psalmist said was simply that they who know God to be the kind of God He is will put their confidence in Him. This is not a special virtue, I repeat, but the normal direction any mind takes when confronted with the fact. We are so made that we trust good character and distrust its opposite. That is why unbelief is so intensely wicked. 'He that believeth not God hath made him a liar' (1 Jn 5:10).

The character of God is the Christian's final ground of assurance and the solution of many, if not most, of his practical religious problems. Some persons, for instance, believe that God answered prayer in Bible times but will not do so today, and others hold that the miracles of olden days can never be repeated. To believe so is to deny or at least to ignore almost everything God has revealed about Himself.

We must remember that God always acts like Himself. He has never at any time anywhere in the vast universe acted otherwise than in character with His infinite perfections. This knowledge should be a warning to the enemies of God, and it cannot but be an immense consolation to His friends.

Though God dwells in the centre of eternal mystery, there need be no uncertainty about how He will act in any situation covered by His promises. These promises are infallible predictions. God will always do what He has promised to do when His conditions are met. And His warnings are no less predictive: 'The ungodly shall not stand in the judgement, nor sinners in the congregation of the righteous' (Ps 1:5).

In the light of all this how vain is the effort to have faith by straining to believe the promises in the Holy Scriptures. A promise is only as good as the one who made it, *but it is as good*, and from this knowledge

springs our assurance. By cultivating the knowledge of
God we at the same time cultivate our faith. Yet while so
doing we look not at our faith but at Christ, its author
and finisher. Thus the gaze of the soul is not in, but out
and up to God. So the health of the soul is secured.

7

The Freedom of the Will

It is inherent in the nature of man that his will must be free. Made in the image of God who is completely free, man must enjoy a measure of freedom. This enables him to select his companions for this world and the next; it enables him to yield his soul to whom he will, to give allegiance to God or the devil, to remain a sinner or become a saint.

And God respects this freedom. God once saw everything that He had made, and behold, it was very good. To find fault with the smallest thing God has made is to find fault with its Maker. It is a false humility that would lament that God wrought but imperfectly when He made man in His own image. Sin excepted, there is nothing in human nature to apologise for. This was confirmed for ever when the Eternal Son became permanently incarnated in human flesh.

So highly does God regard His handiwork that He will not for any reason violate it. For God to override man's freedom and force him to act contrary to his own will would be to make a mockery of the image of God in man. This God will never do.

Our Lord Jesus looked after the rich young ruler as he walked away, but He did not follow him or attempt to coerce him. The dignity of the young man's humanity forbade that his choices should be made for him by another. To remain a man he must make his own moral choices; and Christ knew this and permitted him to go his own chosen way. If his human choice took him at last to hell, at least he went there a man; and it is better for the moral universe that he should do so than that he should be jockeyed to a heaven he did not choose, a soulless, will-less automaton.

God will take nine steps toward us, but He will not take the tenth. He will *incline* us to repent, but He cannot do our repenting for us. It is of the essence of repentance that it can only be done by the one who committed the act to be repented of. God can wait on the sinning man; He can withhold judgement; He can exercise long-suffering to the point where He appears 'lax' in His judicial administration; but He cannot force a man to repent. To do this would be to violate the man's freedom and void the gift God originally bestowed upon him.

Where there is no freedom of choice there can be neither sin nor righteousness, because it is of the nature of both that they be voluntary. However good an act may be, it is not good if it is imposed from without. The act of imposition destroys the moral content of the act and renders it null and void.

For an act to be sinful the quality of voluntariness must also be present. Sin is the voluntary commission of an act known to be contrary to the will of God. Where there is no moral knowledge or where there is no voluntary choice, the act is not sinful; it cannot be, for sin is the transgression of the law and transgression *must* be voluntary.

Lucifer became Satan when he made his fateful choice: 'I will ascend above the heights of the clouds; I will be like the most High.' Clearly here was a choice made against light. Both knowledge and will were present in the act. Conversely, Christ revealed His holiness when He cried in His agony, 'Not my will, but thine, be

done.' Here was a deliberate choice made with the full
knowledge of the consequences. Here two wills were in
temporary conflict, the lower will of the man who was
God and the higher will of the God who was man, and
the higher will prevailed. Here also was seen in glaring
contrast the enormous difference between Christ and
Satan; and that difference divides saint from sinner and
heaven from hell.

But someone may ask, 'When we pray "Not my will,
but Thine be done", are we not voiding our will and
refusing to exercise the very power of choice which is
part of the image of God in us?' The answer to that
question is a flat no, but the whole thing deserves further
explanation.

No act that is done voluntarily is an abrogation of the
freedom of will. If a man *chooses* the will of God he is
not denying but exercising his right of choice. What he is
doing is admitting that he is not good enough to desire
the highest choice nor is he wise enough to make it, and
he is for that reason asking another who is both wise and
good to make his choice for him. And for fallen man this
is the ultimate use he should make of his freedom of will.

Tennyson saw this and wrote of Christ,

> *Thou seemest human and divine,*
> *The highest, holiest manhood, Thou;*
> *Our wills are ours, we know not how;*
> *Our wills are ours, to make them Thine.*

There is a lot of sound doctrine in these words–'Our
wills are ours, to make them Thine.' The secret of saintli-
ness is not the destruction of the will but the sub-
mergence of it in the will of God.

The true saint is one who acknowledges that he possesses from God the gift of freedom. He knows that he
will never be cudgelled into obedience nor wheedled like
a petulant child into doing the will of God; he knows that
these methods are unworthy both of God and of his own

soul. He knows he is free to make any choice he will, and with that knowledge he chooses for ever the blessed will of God.

8

Living an Exchanged Life

A great preacher whom I heard a few years ago said that
the word 'renew' in Isaiah 40:31 really meant 'exchange';
so the text should read, 'They that wait upon the Lord
shall exchange their strength.'

Oddly enough I do not now remember how he
developed his sermon or just how he applied the text,
but I have been thinking lately that the man had hit upon
a very important idea; namely, that a large part of Christian experience consists of exchanging something worse
for something better, a blessed and delightful bargain
indeed.

At the foundation of the Christian life lies vicarious
atonement, which in essence is a transfer of guilt from
the sinner to the Saviour. I well know how vigorously
this idea is attacked by non-Christians, but I also know
that the wise of this world in their pride often miss the
treasures which the simple-hearted find on their knees;
and I also remember the words of the apostle: 'He hath
made him to be sin for us, who knew no sin; that we
might be made the righteousness of God in him' (2 Cor
5:21). This is too plain to miss for anyone who is not
wilfully blind: Christ by His death on the cross made it
possible for the sinner to exchange his sin for Christ's

righteousness. It's that simple. No one is compelled to accept it, but at least that is what it means.

And that is only the beginning. Almost everything thereafter is an exchange of the worse for the better. Next after the exchange of sin for righteousness is that of wrath for acceptance. Today the wrath of God abides upon a sinning and impenitent man; tomorrow God's smile rests upon him. He is the same man, but not quite, for he is now a new man in Christ Jesus. By penitence and faith he has exchanged the place of condemnation for the Father's house. He was rejected in himself but is now accepted in the Beloved, and this not by human means but by an act of divine grace.

Then comes the exchange of death for life. Christ died for dead men that they might rise to be living men. Paul's happy if somewhat involved testimony makes this clear: 'I am crucified with Christ: nevertheless I live; yet not I, but Christ liveth in me: and the life which I now live in the flesh I live by the faith of the Son of God, who loved me, and gave himself for me' (Gal 2:20).

This is mysterious but not incredible. It is one more example of how the ways of God and the ways of man diverge. Man is a born cobbler. When he wants a thing to be better he goes to work to improve it. He improves cattle by careful breeding; cars and planes by streamlining; health by diet, vitamins and surgery; plants by grafting; people by education. But God will have none of this cobbling. He makes a man better by making him a new man, He imparts a higher order of life and sets to work to destroy the old.

Then as suggested in the Isaiah text, the Christian exchanges weakness for strength. I suppose it is not improper to say that God makes His people strong, but we must understand this to mean that they become strong in exact proportion to their weakness, the weakness being their own and the strength God's. 'When I am weak, then am I strong' is the way Paul said it and in so saying set a pattern for every Christian.

Actually the purest saint at the moment of his greatest strength is as weak as he was before his conversion. What has happened is that he has switched from his little human battery to the infinite power of God. He has quite literally exchanged weakness for strength, but the strength is not his; it flows into him from God as long as he abides in Christ.

One of the heaviest problems in the Christian life is that of sanctification: how to become as pure as we know we ought to be and must be if we are to enjoy intimate communion with a holy God. The classic expression of this problem and its solution is found in Paul's Epistle to the Romans, chapters seven and eight. The cry, 'O wretched man that I am! who shall deliver me from the body of this death?' (Rom 7:24) receives the triumphant answer, 'The law of the Spirit of life in Christ Jesus hath made me free from the law of sin and death' (Rom 8:2).

No one who has given attention to the facts will deny that it is altogether possible for a man to attain to a high degree of external morality if he sets his heart to it. Marcus Aurelius, the pagan emperor, for instance, lived a life of such exalted morality as to make most of us Christians ashamed, as did also the lowly slave Epictetus; but holiness was something of which they were totally ignorant. And it is holiness that the Christian heart yearns far above all else, and holiness the human heart can never capture by itself.

A. B. Simpson knew by experience the unavailing struggle to be holy, and he knew also the Bible way to holiness. In a little hymn composed to be spoken at the conclusion of one of his sermons he states it this way:

> I take Him as my holiness,
>   My spirit's spotless, heavenly dress;
> I take "The Lord my righteousness",
>   I take, He undertakes.

We have but to abandon the effort to be holy and trust God to do the work within us. He will surely undertake.

There are many other happy exchanges we Christians may make if we will, among them being our ignorance for His knowledge, our folly for His wisdom, our demerit for His merit, our sad mortality for His blessed immortality and faith for sight at last.

9

Why the Holy Spirit Is Given

A generation ago the work of the Holy Spirit in the life of the believer was neatly reduced by certain Bible teachers to one thing: to impart power for service.

In the first quarter of the present century the phrase 'power for service' occurred everywhere in the literature of evangelical Christianity, and one gets the distinct impression that it was meant to serve as a biblical reason for the presence of the Holy Spirit in the church other than that advanced by the charismatic sects which about that time were going big in various parts of the world, especially in the United States. These claimed that they had returned to basic New Testament Christianity and offered as proof the presence of the Spirit's gifts among them, with particular, one might say exclusive, emphasis on the gift of tongues. This teaching was accompanied by a great outburst of emotionalism. Those who had the experience enjoyed it immensely and the onlookers could not but be deeply affected by this demonstration of joy.

The more staid members of the evangelical community could not go along with the emotionalism of the Pentecostalists nor with the obvious lack of balance in their theology and lack of responsibility in their general conduct. But the matter of the Spirit had to be dealt with. The popular Bible teachers came up with the 'power for service' doctrine and a lot of good people were greatly relieved. According to this counter-doctrine, the infilling of the Spirit is necessary and altogether to be desired, but for reasons other than those advanced by the Pentecostalists. The one great work of the Spirit in the life of the believer, they said, is to impart 'power for service'. Thus it is not emotional or charismatic but practical. The Christian is weak and the Spirit is given to make him strong so that he can serve effectively. This view was supported by Acts 1:8: 'Ye shall receive power, after that the Holy Ghost is come upon you: and ye shall be witnesses unto me.'

Now I have often tried to make the point that truths that are compelled to stand alone never stand straight and are not likely to stand long. Truth is one but truths are many. Scriptural truths are interlocking and interdependent. A trust is rarely valid in isolation. A statement may be true in its relation to other truths and less than true when separated from them. 'The truth, the whole truth, and nothing but the truth' is good not only for a court of law but for the pulpit, the classroom and the prayer chamber as well.

To teach that the filling with the Holy Spirit is given to the Christian to provide 'power for service' is to teach truth, but not the whole truth. Power for service is but one effect of the experience, and I do not hesitate to say that it is the least of several effects. It is least for the very reason that it touches service, presumably service to mankind; and contrary to the popular belief, 'to serve this present age' is not the Christian's first duty nor the chief end of man.

As I have stated elsewhere, the two great verbs that dominate the life of man are *be* and *do*. What a man *is* comes first in the sight of God. What he does is determined by what he is, so *is* is of first importance always. The modern notion that we are 'saved to serve', while true, is true only in a wider context, and as understood by busy Christians today it is not true at all.

Redemption became necessary not because of what men were doing only, but because of what they were. Not human conduct alone had gone wrong but human nature as well; apart from the moral defect in human nature no evil conduct would have occurred. Fallen men acted in accord with what they were. Their hearts dictated their deeds. 'And God saw that the wickedness of man was great in the earth' (Gen 6:5). That much any moral being could have seen. But God saw more; He saw the cause of man's wicked ways, and that 'every imagination of the thoughts of his heart was only evil continually'. The stream of human conduct flows out of a fountain polluted by evil thoughts and imaginations.

To purge the stream it was necessary to purify the fountain; and to reform human conduct it is necessary to regenerate human nature. The fundamental *be* must be sanctified if we would have a righteous *do,* for being and doing are related as cause and effect, as father and son.

The primary work of the Holy Spirit is to restore the lost soul to intimate fellowship with God through the washing of regeneration. To accomplish this He first reveals Christ to the penitent heart (1 Cor 12:3). He then goes on to illumine the newborn soul with brighter rays from the face of Christ (Jn 14:26; 16:13–15) and leads the willing heart into depths and heights of divine knowledge and communion. Remember, we know Christ only as the Spirit enables us and we have only as much of Him as the Holy Spirit imparts.

God wants worshippers before workers; indeed the only acceptable workers are those who have learned the lost art of worship. It is inconceivable that a sovereign and holy God should be so hard up for workers that He would press into service anyone who had been empowered regardless of his moral qualifications. The very stones would praise Him if the need arose and a thousand legions of angels would leap to do His will.

Gifts and power for service the Spirit surely desires to impart; but holiness and spiritual worship come first.

10

God Walking Among Men

God always acts like Himself, wherever He may be and whatever He may be doing; in Him there is neither variableness nor shadow of turning. Yet His infinitude places Him so far above our knowing that a lifetime spent in cultivating the knowledge of Him leaves as much yet to learn as if we had never begun.

God's limitless knowledge and perfect wisdom enable Him to work rationally beyond the bounds of our rational knowing. For this reason we cannot predict God's actions as we can predict the movements of the heavenly bodies, so He constantly astonishes us as He moves in freedom through His universe. So imperfectly do we know Him that it may be said that one invariable concomitant of a true encounter with God is delighted wonder. No matter how high our expectation may be, when God finally moves into the field of our spiritual awareness we are sure to be astonished by His power to overwhelm the mind and fascinate the soul. He is always more wonderful than we anticipate, and more blessed and marvellous than we had imagined He could be.

Yet in a measure His actions may be predicted, for, as I have said, He always acts like Himself. Since we know, for instance, that God is love, we may be perfectly sure that love will be present in His every act, whether it be the salvation of a penitent sinner or the destruction of an impenitent world. Similarly we can know that He will always be just, faithful, merciful and true.

It is a rare mind, I suppose, that is much concerned with the conduct of God in those distant realms that lie beyond human experience. But almost everyone has wondered how God would act if He were in our place. And we may have had moments when we felt that God could not possibly understand how hard it is for us to live right in such an evil world as this. And we may have wondered how He would act and what He would do if He were to live among us for a while.

To wonder thus may be natural but it is wholly needless. We know how God would act if He were in our place—*He has been in our place*. It is the mystery of godliness that God was manifest in human flesh. They called His name Emmanuel, which being interpreted is *God with us* (Matt 1:23).

When Jesus walked on earth He was a man acting like God; but equally wonderful is it that He was also God acting like Himself in man and in a man. We know how God acts in heaven because we saw Him act on earth. 'He that hath seen me hath seen the Father; and how sayest thou then, Show us the Father?'

As glorious as this is, it does not end there. God is still walking in men, and wherever He walks He acts like Himself. This is not poetry but plain, hard fact capable of being tested in the laboratory of life.

That Christ actually inhabits the nature of the regenerate believer is assumed, implied and overtly stated in the Holy Scriptures. All the persons of the Godhead are said to enter the nature of the one that engages New Testament truth in faith and obedience. 'If a man love me, he will keep my words: and my Father will love him, and we will come unto him, and make our abode with him' (Jn 14:23). And the doctrine of the indwelling of the Holy Spirit is too well known to need support here; everyone that is taught even slightly in the Word of God understands this.

Whatever God is the man Christ Jesus is also. It has been the firm belief of the Church from the days of the apostles that God is not only manifest in Christ but that He is manifest *as* Christ. In the days of the Arian controversy the church fathers were driven to put the teaching of the New Testament on this subject into a highly condensed 'rule' or creed which might be accepted as final by all believers. This they did in the following words: 'The right faith is that we believe and confess that our Lord Jesus Christ, the Son of God, is God and Man. God of the substance of His Father, begotten before all ages: Man of the substance of His mother, born in the world. Perfect God and perfect Man.... As the reasonable soul and flesh is one man: so God and man is one Christ.'

Christ in a believer's heart will act the same as He acted in Galilee and Judea. His disposition is the same now as then. He was holy, righteous, compassionate, meek and humble then, and He has not changed. He is the same wherever He is found, whether it be at the right hand of God or in the nature of a true disciple. He was friendly, loving, prayerful, kindly, worshipful, self-sacrificing while walking among men; is it not reasonable to expect Him to be the same when walking *in* men?

Why then do true Christians sometimes act in an unChristlike manner? Some would assume that when a professed Christian fails to show forth the moral beauty of Christ in his life it is a proof that he has been deceived and is actually not a real Christian at all. But the explanation is not so simple as that.

The truth is that while Christ dwells in the believer's new nature, He has strong competition from the believer's old nature. The warfare between the old and the new goes on continually in most believers. This is accepted as inevitable, but the New Testament does not so teach. A prayerful study of Romans 6 to 8 points the way to victory. If Christ is allowed complete sway He will live in us as He lived in Galilee.

11

The Divine Indwelling

The doctrine of the divine indwelling is one of the most important in the New Testament, and its meaning for the individual Christian is precious beyond all description. To neglect it is to suffer serious loss. The apostle Paul prayed for the Ephesian Christians that Christ might dwell in their hearts by faith. Surely it takes faith of a more than average vitality to grasp the full implications of this great truth.

Two facts join to make the doctrine difficult to accept: the supreme greatness of God and the utter sinfulness of man. Those who think poorly of God and well of themselves may chatter idly of 'the deity within', but the man who trembles before the high and lofty one that inhabiteth eternity, whose name is Holy, the man who knows the depth of his own sin, will detect a moral incongruity in the teaching that one so holy should dwell in the heart of one so vile.

But however incongruous it may appear to be, in the Holy Scriptures it is taught so fully that it cannot be overlooked and so plainly that it can hardly be misunderstood. 'If a man love me,' said our Lord Jesus Christ, 'he will keep my words: and my Father will love him, and we will come unto him, and make our abode with him' (Jn 14:23). That this abiding is *within the man* is shown by these words: 'At that day ye shall know that I am in my Father, and ye in me, and I in you' (verse 20). Christ said of the Holy Spirit: 'He...shall be in you' (verse 17), and in His great prayer in John 17 our Lord twice used the words 'I in them'.

The truth of the divine indwelling is developed more fully in the epistles of Paul. 'Know ye not that ye are the temple of God, and that the Spirit of God dwelleth in you?...For the temple of God is holy, which temple ye are' (1 Cor 3:16, 17). And again (1 Cor 6:19), 'What? know ye not that your body is the temple of the Holy Ghost which is in you, which ye have of God, and ye are not your own?'

Without question, the teaching of the New Testament is that the very God Himself inhabits the nature of His true children. How this can be I do not know, but neither do I know how my soul inhabits my body. Paul called this wonder of the indwelling God a rich mystery: 'Christ in you, the hope of glory!' And if the doctrine involved a contradiction or even an impossibility we must still believe what the mouth of the Lord has spoken. 'Yea, let God be true, but every man a liar' (Rom 3:4).

The spiritual riches lying buried in this truth are so vast that they are worth any care or effort we may give to their recovery. Yet we are not concerned primarily with the theology or metaphysics embodied here. We want to know the reality of it. What does the truth mean to us in practical out-working? What does it have for a serious-minded Christian compelled to live in a dark and godless world? As Paul would say, 'Much every way.'

God does not dwell passively in His people; He *wills* and *works* in them (Phil 2:13); and remember, wherever He is, God always acts like Himself. He will do in us whatever His holy nature moves Him to do; and unless He is hindered by our resistance He will act in us precisely as He acts in heaven. Only an unsanctified human will can prevent Him.

Without doubt we hinder God greatly by our wilfulness and our unbelief. We fail to co-operate with the holy impulses of the in-living Spirit; we go contrary to His will as it is revealed in the Scriptures, either because we have not taken time to discover what the Bible teaches or because we do not approve it when we do.

This contest between the indwelling Deity and our own fallen propensities occupies a large place in New Testament theology. But the warfare need not continue indefinitely. Christ has made full provision for our deliverance from the bondage of the flesh. A frank and realistic presentation of the whole thing is set forth in Romans 6 and 7, and in the eighth chapter a triumphant solution is discovered: It is, briefly, through a spiritual crucifixion with Christ followed by resurrection and an infusion of the Holy Spirit.

Once the heart is freed from its contrary impulses, Christ within becomes a wondrous experiential fact. The surrendered heart has no more controversy with God, so He can live in us congenial and uninhibited. Then He thinks His own thoughts in us: thoughts about ourselves, about Himself, about sinners and saints and babes and harlots; thoughts about the church, about sin and judgement and hell and heaven. And He thinks about us and Himself and His love for us and our love for Him; and He woos us to Himself as a bridegroom woos his bride.

Yet there is nothing formal or automatic about His operations within us. We are personalities and we are engaged with personality. We are intelligent and have wills of our own. We can, so to speak, stand outside of ourselves and discipline ourselves into accord with the will of God. We can commune with our own hearts upon our beds and be still. We can talk to our God in the night watches. We can learn what He wants us to be, and pray and work to prepare Him a habitation.

And what kind of habitation pleases God? What must our natures be like before He can feel at home within us? He asks nothing but a pure heart and a single mind. He asks no rich panelling, no rugs from the Orient, no art treasures from afar. He desires but sincerity, transparency, humility and love. He will see to the rest.

12

We Are Saved *To* as well as *From*

The evangelical church today is in the awkward position of being wrong while it is right, and a little preposition makes the difference.

I think there can be no question but that if we let the Bible decide right and wrong the evangelicals are right in their creedal position. Even the sceptic H. L. Mencken said, 'If the Bible is true, the fundamentalists are right.' He did not grant the truth of the Bible, but he was sharp enough to see that the basic doctrines taught by fundamentalists were identical with those taught by the Bible.

One place where we are wrong while we are right is in the relative stress we lay upon the prepositions *to* and *from* when they follow the word *saved*. For a long generation we have been holding the letter of truth while at the same time we have been moving away from it in spirit because we have been preoccupied with what we are saved *from* rather than what we have been saved *to*.

The right relative importance of the two concepts is set forth by Paul in his first epistle to the Thessalonians: 'Ye turned to God from idols to serve the living and true God; and to wait for his Son from heaven.'

The Christian is saved from his past sins. With these he simply has nothing more to do; they are among the things to be forgotten as the night is forgotten at the

52

dawning of the day. He is also saved from the wrath to come. With this also he has nothing to do. It exists, but not for him. Sin and wrath have a cause and effect relationship, and because for the Christian sin is cancelled wrath is cancelled also. The 'froms' of the Christian life concern negatives, and to be engrossed in them is to live in a state of negation. Yet that is where many earnest believers live most of the time.

We are not called to fellowship with non-existence. We are called to things that exist in truth, to positive things, and it is as we become occupied with these that health comes to the soul. Spiritual life cannot feed on negatives. The man who is constantly reciting the evils of his unconverted days is looking in the wrong direction. He is like a man trying to run a race while looking back over his shoulder.

What the Christian used to be is altogether the least important thing about him. What he is yet to be is all that should concern him. He may occasionally, as Paul sometimes did, remember to his own shame the life he once lived; but that should be only a quick glance; it is never to be a fixed gaze. Our long permanent look is on God and the glory that shall be revealed.

What we are saved *from* and what we are saved *to* bear the same relation to each other as a serious illness and recovered health. The physician should stand between these two opposites to save from one and restore to the other. Once the great sickness is cured the memory of it should be thrust out onto the margin of the mind to grow fainter and weaker as it retreats farther away; and the fortunate man whose health has been restored should go on to use his new strength to accomplish something useful for mankind.

Yet many persons permit their sick bodies to condition their mental stuff so that after the body has become well they still retain the old feeling of chronic invalidism they had before. They are recovered, true enough, but not *to* anything. We have but to imagine a group of such persons testifying every Sunday about their late illnesses and singing plaintive songs about them and we have a pretty fair picture of many gatherings among Christians today.

There is an art of forgetting, and every Christian should become skilled in it. Forgetting the things which are behind is a positive necessity if we are to become more than mere babes in Christ. If we cannot trust God to have dealt effectually with our past we may as well throw in the sponge now and have it over with. Fifty years of grieving over our sins cannot blot out their guilt. But if God has indeed pardoned and cleansed us, then we should count it done and waste no more time in sterile lamentations.

And thank God this sudden obliteration of our familiar past does not leave us with a vacuum. Far from it. Into the empty world vacated by our sins and failures rushes the blessed Spirit of God, bringing with Him everything new. New life, new hope, new enjoyments, new interests, new purposeful toil, and best of all a new and satisfying object toward which to direct our soul's enraptured gaze. God now fills the recovered garden, and we may without fear walk and commune with Him in the cool of the day.

Right here is where the weakness of much current Christianity lies. We have not learned where to lay our emphasis. Particularly we have not understood that we are saved to know God, to enter His wonder-filled presence through the new and living way and remain in that presence for ever. We are called to an everlasting preoccupation with God. The Triune God with all of His mystery and majesty is ours and we are His, and eternity will not be long enough to experience all that He is of goodness, holiness and truth.

In heaven they rest not day or night in their ecstatic worship of the Godhead. We profess to be headed for that place; shall we not begin now to worship on earth as we shall do in heaven?

13

Will and Emotion in the Christian Life

Emotion, says Drever's *Dictionary of Psychology*, is a state of excitement or perturbation, marked by strong feeling and usually an impulse toward a definite form of behaviour.

'Excitement, perturbation, feeling.' These are states of mind we are all familiar with. In a world as violent and full of conflict as this these come and go, blaze up and die down in the average man's bosom a hundred times a day. The normal man and woman will in the course of a few months experience every degree of emotion from near ecstasy to mild dejection without apparently being any the better or the worse for it. Of course I have in mind here only the normal man and woman. The psychopathic personality lies outside the field of this study.

The emotions are neither to be feared nor despised, for they are a normal part of us as God made us in the first place. Indeed the full human life would be impossible without them. One recoils from the thought of the man who lacked all feeling. He would be either a cold, naked intellect such as inhabits the pages of the science-fiction novel, or a mere vegetable, such as is sometimes found in the incurable wards of our mental hospitals.

The right relation of intellect to feeling and feeling to will is disclosed in Matthew 14:14. 'And Jesus went forth, and saw a great multitude, and was moved with compassion toward them, and he healed their sick.' Intellectual knowledge of the suffering of the people stirred His pity and His pity moved Him to heal them. This is how it was with the ideal man whose total organism was perfectly adjusted to itself; and this is the way it is with us in a less perfect measure.

A state of emotion always comes between the knowledge and the act. A feeling of pity would never arise in the human breast unless aroused by a mental picture of others' distress, and without the emotional bump to set off the will there would be no act of mercy. That is the way we are constituted. Whether the emotion aroused by a mental picture be pity, love, fear, desire, grief, there can be no act of the will without it. What I am saying here is nothing new. Every mother, every statesman, every leader of men, every preacher of the Word of God knows that a mental picture must be presented to the listener before he can be moved to act, even though it be for his own advantage.

God intended that truth should move us to moral action. The mind receives ideas, mental pictures of things as they are. These excite the feelings and these in turn move the will to act in accordance with the truth. That is the way it should be, and would be had not sin entered and wrought injury to our inner life. Because of sin the simple sequence of truth–feeling–action may break down in any of its three parts. The mind which is created to receive truth is often turned over to falsehood, and the feelings thus aroused may incite the will to evil action. The contemplation of any wrong or forbidden thing cannot but inflame the feelings to sympathy with evil.

A regrettable example of this was David's long gaze at the beautiful Bathsheba in the act of bathing. The king was moved by what he saw and acted accordingly, and the bitter and tragic consequences dogged him to the end of his days. He saw, he felt, he acted, precisely as his

Lord did centuries later when He healed the sick. The difference in the moral quality of the acts of the two men resulted from the difference in their feelings, and these were the result of the objects that aroused the feelings. David saw a beautiful woman; Christ saw a suffering multitude. One gaze led to sin, the other to an act of mercy; but both followed the simple law of their inner structure.

Another breakdown in the truth–feeling–act sequence comes when the heart for selfish reasons deliberately hardens itself against the Word of God. This is the state of all who love darkness rather than light and for that reason either withdraw from the light altogether or when exposed to it stubbornly refuse to obey it. The covetous man looks on human need and sternly refuses to be moved by it. To yield to the impulse of generosity naturally aroused by the sight of poverty would require him to give up some of his cherished hoard, and this he will not do. So the fountain of generosity is frozen at its source. The miser keeps his gold, the poor man suffers on in his poverty and the whole course of nature is upset. Is it any wonder that God hates covetousness?

But be sure that human feelings can never be completely stifled. If they are forbidden their normal course, like a river they will cut another channel through the life and flow out to curse and ruin and destroy.

The Christian who gazes too long on the carnal pleasures of this world cannot escape a certain feeling of sympathy with them, and that feeling will inevitably lead to behaviour that is worldly. And to expose our hearts to truth and consistently refuse or neglect to obey the impulses it arouses is to stymie the motions of life within us and, if persisted in, to grieve the Holy Spirit into silence.

The Scriptures and our own human constitution agree to teach us to love truth and to obey the sweet impulses of righteousness it raises within us. If we love our own souls we dare do nothing else.

14

How to Avoid Serious Error

There are areas of Christian thought, and because of thought then also of life, where likenesses and differences are so difficult to distinguish that we are often hard put to it to escape complete deception.

Throughout the whole world error and truth travel the same highways, work in the same fields and factories, attend the same churches, fly in the same planes and shop in the same stores. So skilled is error at imitating truth that the two are constantly being mistaken for each other. It takes a sharp eye these days to know which brother is Cain and which Abel.

We must never take for granted anything that touches our soul's welfare. Isaac felt Jacob's arms and thought they were the arms of Esau. Even the disciples failed to spot the traitor among them; the only one of them who knew who he was was Judas himself. That soft-spoken companion with whom we walk so comfortably and in whose company we take such delight may be an angel of Satan, whereas that rough, plain-spoken man whom we shun may be God's very prophet sent to warn us against danger and eternal loss.

It is therefore critically important that the Christian take full advantage of every provision God has made to save him from delusion. These are *prayer, faith, constant meditation on the Scriptures, obedience, humility, hard, serious thought and the illumination of the Holy Spirit.*

1. Prayer is not a sure fire protection against error for the reason that there are many kinds of prayer and some of them are worse than useless. The prophets of Baal leapt upon the altar in a frenzy of prayer, but their cries went unregarded because they prayed to a god that did not exist. The God the Pharisees prayed to did exist, but He refused to listen to them because of their self-righteousness and pride. From them we may well learn a profitable lesson in reverse.

In spite of the difficulties we encounter when we pray, prayer is a powerful and effective way to get right, stay right and stay free from error. 'If any of you lack wisdom, let him ask of God, that giveth to all men liberally, and upbraideth not; and it shall be given him' (Js 1:5). All things else being equal, the praying man is less likely to think wrong than the man who neglects to pray. 'Men ought always to pray, and not to faint' (Lk 18:1).

2. The apostle Paul calls faith a shield. The man of faith can walk at ease, protected by his simple confidence in God. God loves to be trusted, and He puts all heaven at the disposal of the trusting soul.

But when we talk of faith let us know what we mean. Faith is not optimism, though it may breed optimism; it is not cheerfulness, though the man of faith is likely to be reasonably cheerful; it is not a vague sense of well-being or a tender appreciation for the beauty of human togetherness. Faith is confidence in God's self-revelation as found in the Holy Scriptures.

3. 'Faith cometh by hearing, and hearing by the word of God.' The Scriptures purify, instruct, strengthen, enlighten and inform. The blessed man will meditate in them day and night.

4. To be entirely safe from the devil's snares the man of God must be completely obedient to the Word of the Lord. The driver on the highway is safe, not when he

reads the signs but when he obeys them. So it is with the Scriptures. To be effective they must be obeyed.

5. Again, there is a close relation between humility and the perception of truth. 'The meek will he guide in judgement: and the meek will he teach his way' (Ps 25:9). In the Scriptures I find no shred of encouragement for the proud. Only the tame sheep can be led; only the humble child need expect the guidance of the Father's hand. When all the evidence is in it may well be found that none but the proud ever strayed from the truth and that self-trust was behind every heresy that ever afflicted the church.

6. Then we must think. Human thought has its limitations, but where there is no thinking there is not likely to be any large deposit of truth in the mind. Evangelicals at the moment appear to be divided into two camps–those who trust the human intellect to the point of sheer rationalism, and those who are shy of everything intellectual and are convinced that thinking is a waste of the Christian's time.

Surely both are wrong. Self-conscious intellectualism is offensive to man and, I am convinced, to God also but it is significant that every major revelation in the Scriptures was made to a man of superior intellect. It would be easy to marshall an imposing list of biblical quotations exhorting us to think, but a more convincing argument is the whole drift of the Bible itself. The Scriptures simply take for granted that the saints of the Most High will be serious-minded, thoughtful persons. They never leave the impression that it is sinful to think.

7. But thinking apart from the inward illumination of the Holy Spirit is not only futile, it is likely to be dangerous as well. The human intellect is fallen and can no more find its way through the broad expanse of truth, half-truth and downright error than a ship can find its way over the ocean alone. God has given us the Holy Spirit to illuminate our minds. He is eyes and understanding to us. We dare not try to get on without Him.

15

Our Tendency Toward Religious Lopsidedness

It is a thin and rather smooth coin of common knowledge that the human race has lost its symmetry and tends to be lopsided in almost everything it is and does. Religious philosophers have recognised this asymmetry and have sought to correct it by preaching in one form or another the doctrine of the 'golden mean'. Confucius taught the 'middle way'; Buddha would have his followers avoid both asceticism and bodily ease; Aristotle believed that the virtuous life is the one perfectly balanced between excess and defect.

Christianity, being in full accord with all the facts of existence, takes into account this moral imbalance in human life, and the remedy it offers is not a new philosophy but a new life. The ideal to which the Christian aspires is not to walk in the perfect way but to be transformed by the renewing of his mind and conformed to the likeness of Christ.

The regenerate man often has a more difficult time of it than the unregenerate, for he is not one man but two. He feels within him a power that tends toward holiness and God, while at the same time he is still a child of Adam's flesh and a son of the red clay. This moral dualism is to him a source of distress and struggle wholly unknown to the once-born man. Of course the classic critique upon this is Paul's testimony in the seventh chapter of his Roman epistle.

The true Christian is a saint in embryo. The heavenly genes are in him and the Holy Spirit is working to bring him on into a spiritual development that accords with the nature of the Heavenly Father from whom he received the deposit of divine life. Yet he is here in this mortal body subject to weakness and temptation, and his warfare with the flesh sometimes leads him to do extreme things. 'For the flesh lusteth against the Spirit, and the Spirit against the flesh: and these are contrary the one to the other: so that ye cannot do the things that ye would' (Gal 5:17).

The work of the Spirit in the human heart is not an unconscious or automatic thing. Human will and intelligence must yield to and co-operate with the benign intentions of God. I think it is here that many of us go astray. Either we try to make ourselves holy and fail miserably, as we certainly must; or we seek to achieve a state of spiritual passivity and wait for God to perfect our natures in holiness as one might sit down and wait for a robin egg to hatch or a rose to burst into bloom. So we work feverishly to do the impossible or we do not work at all; and there lies the asymmetry about which I write.

The New Testament knows nothing of the working of the Spirit in us apart from our own moral responses. Watchfulness, prayer, self-discipline and intelligent acquiescence in the purposes of God are indispensable to any real progress in holiness.

There are areas in our lives where in our effort to be right we may go wrong, so wrong as to lead to spiritual deformity. To be specific let me name a few:

1. *When in our determination to be bold we become brazen.* Courage and meekness are compatible qualities: both were found in perfect proportion in Christ and both shone in beauty in His conflict with His enemies. Peter before the Sanhedrin and Paul before Agrippa demonstrated both qualities, though on another occasion when

Paul's boldness temporarily lost its charity and became carnal he said to the high priest, 'God shall smite thee, thou whited wall.' It is to the credit of the apostle that when he saw what he had done he immediately apologised (Acts 23:1–5).

2. *When in our desire to be frank we become rude.* Candour without rudeness was always found in the man Christ Jesus. The Christian who boasts that he always calls a spade a spade is likely to end by calling everything a spade. Even the fiery Peter learned that love does not blurt out everything it knows (1 Pet 4:8).

3. *When in our effort to be watchful we become suspicious.* Because there are many adversaries the temptation is to see enemies where none exist. Because we are in conflict with error we tend to develop a spirit of hostility to everyone who disagrees with us on anything. Satan cares little whether we go astray after a false doctrine or merely turn sour. Either way he wins.

4. *When we seek to be serious and become sombre.* The saints have always been serious, but gloominess is a defect of character and should never be equated with godliness. Religious melancholy may indicate the presence of unbelief or sin and if long continued may lead to serious mental disturbance. Joy is a great therapeutic for the mind. 'Rejoice in the Lord alway' (Phil 4:4).

5. *When we mean to be conscientious and become over-scrupulous.* If the devil cannot succeed in destroying the conscience he will settle for making it sick. I know Christians who live in a state of constant distress, fearing that they may displease God. Their world of permitted acts becomes narrower year by year till at last they fear to engage in the common pursuits of life. They believe this self-torture to be a proof of godliness, but how wrong they are.

These are but a few examples of serious imbalance in the Christian life. I trust the remedy has been suggested as we went along.

16

The Need for Divine Illumination

Spiritual truths differ from natural truths both in their constitution and in the manner of their apprehension by us.

Natural truths can be learned by us regardless of our moral or spiritual condition. The truths of the natural sciences, for instance, can be grasped by anyone of normal intelligence regardless of whether he is a good man or a scoundrel. There is no relation between, say, chastity and logic, or between kindness and oceanography. In like manner a sufficient degree of mental vigour is all that is required to grasp philosophical propositions. A man may study philosophy for a lifetime, teach it, write books about it, and be all the while proud, covetous and thoroughly dishonest in his private dealings.

The same thing may be said of theology. A man need not be godly to learn theology. Indeed I wonder whether there is anything taught in any seminary on earth that could not be learned by a brigand or a swindler as well as by a consecrated Christian. While I have no doubt that the majority of theological students live far better than average lives, yet it should be kept in mind that they can easily get their lessons without living any better than is absolutely required to stay in the institution.

It does not strain my imagination to think of Judas

Iscariot as coming out of school with a B.D., if such a thing had been offered in his day. There is simply no necessary relation between the studies engaged in by students in a divinity school and the state of the students' hearts. Anything that is taught under the heading of soteriology, eschatology, pneumatology or any of the rest may be grasped as easily by a sinner as by a saint. And certainly it takes no great degree of sanctity to learn Hebrew and Greek.

Surely God has that to say to the pure in heart which He cannot say to the man of sinful life. But what He has to say is not theological, it is spiritual; and right there lies the weight of my argument. Spiritual truths cannot be received in the ordinary way of nature. 'The natural man receiveth not the things of the Spirit of God: for they are foolishness unto him: neither can he know them, because they are spiritually discerned.' So wrote the apostle Paul to the believers at Corinth.

Our Lord referred to this kind of Spirit-enlightened knowledge many times. To Him it was the fruit of a divine illumination, not contrary to but altogether beyond mere intellectual light. The fourth Gospel is full of this idea; indeed the idea is so important to the understanding of John's Gospel that anyone who denies it might as well give up trying to grasp our Lord's teachings as given by the apostle John. And the same idea is found in John's First Epistle, making that epistle extremely difficult to understand but also making it one of the most beautiful and rewarding of all the epistles of the New Testament when its teachings are spiritually discerned.

The necessity for spiritual illumination before we can grasp spiritual truths is taught throughout the entire New Testament and is altogether in accord with the teachings of the Psalms, the Proverbs and the Prophets. The Old Testament Apocrypha agrees with the Scriptures here, and while the Apocryphal books are not to be received as divinely inspired, they are useful as showing how the best minds of ancient Israel thought about this matter of divine truth and how it is received into the human heart.

The New Testament draws a sharp line between the natural mind and the mind that has been touched by divine fire. When Peter made his good confession, 'Thou art the Christ, the Son of the living God,' our Lord replied, 'Blessed art thou, Simon Bar-jona: for flesh and blood hath not revealed it unto thee, but my Father which is in heaven.' And Paul expresses much the same thing when he says, 'No man can say that Jesus is the Lord, but by the Holy Ghost.'

The sum of what I am saying is that there is an illumination, divinely bestowed, without which theological truth is information and nothing more. While this illumination is never given apart from theology, it is entirely possible to have theology without the illumination. This results in what has been called 'dead orthodoxy', and while there may be some who deny that it is possible to be both orthodox and dead at the same time I am afraid experience proves that it is.

Revivals, as they have appeared at various times among the churches of the past, have been essentially a quickening of the spiritual life of persons already orthodox. The revivalist, as long as he exercised his ministry as a revivalist, did not try to teach doctrine. His one object was to bring about a quickening of the churches which while orthodox in creed were devoid of spiritual life. When he went beyond this he was something other than a revivalist. Revival can come only to those who know truth. When the inner meaning of familiar doctrines suddenly flashes in upon the heart of a Christian the revival for him has already begun. It may go on to be much more than this but it can never be less.

17

Truth Has Two Wings

Truth is like a bird; it cannot fly on one wing. Yet we are for ever trying to take off with one wing flapping furiously and the other tucked neatly out of sight.

I believe it was Dr G. Campbell Morgan who said that the whole truth does not lie in 'It is written', but in 'It is written' and 'Again it is written'. The second text must be placed over against the first to balance it and give it symmetry, just as the right wing must work along with the left to balance the bird and enable it to fly.

Many of the doctrinal divisions among the churches are the result of a blind and stubborn insistence that truth has but one wing. Each side holds tenaciously to one text, refusing grimly to acknowledge the validity of the other. This error is an evil among churches, but it is a real tragedy when it gets into the hearts of individual Christians and begins to affect their devotional lives.

Lack of balance in the Christian life is often the direct consequence of over-emphasis on certain favourite texts, with a corresponding underemphasis on other related ones. For it is not denial only that makes a truth void; failure to emphasise it will in the long run be equally damaging. And this puts us in the odd position of holding a truth theoretically while we make it of no effect by neglecting it in practice. Unused truth becomes as use-less as an unused muscle.

Sometimes our dogmatic insistence upon 'It is written' and our refusal to hear 'Again it is written' makes heretics of us, our heresy being the non-creedal variety which does not rouse the opposition of the theologians. One example of this is the teaching that crops up now and again having to do with confession of sin. It goes like this: Christ died for our sins, not only for all we have committed but all we may yet commit for the remainder of our lives. When we accept Christ we receive the benefit of everything He did for us in His dying and rising again. In Christ all our current sins are forgiven beforehand. It is therefore unnecessary for us to confess our sins. In Christ they are already forgiven.

Now, this is completely wrong, and it is all the more wrong because it is half right. It is true that Christ died for *all* our sins, but it is not true that because Christ died for all our sins we need not confess that we have sinned when we have. This conclusion does not follow from that premise.

It is written that Christ died for our sins, and again it is written that 'if we confess our sins, he is faithful and just to forgive us our sins' (1 Jn 1:9). These two texts are written of the same company of persons, namely Christians. We dare not compel the first text to invalidate the second. Both are true and one completes the other. The meaning of the two is that since Christ died for our sins if we confess our sins they will be forgiven. To teach otherwise is to attempt to fly on one wing.

Another example: I have met some who claim that it is wrong to pray for the same thing twice, the reason being that if we truly believe when we pray we have the answer the first time; any second prayer betrays the unbelief of the first; *ergo*, let there be no second prayer.

There are three things wrong with this teaching. One is that it ignores a large body of Scripture; the second is that it rarely works in practice, even for the saintliest soul; and the third is that, if persisted in, it robs the praying man of two of his mightiest weapons in his warfare with the flesh and the devil, viz., intercession and petition.

For let it be said without qualification that the effective intercessor is never a one-prayer man, neither does the successful petitioner win his mighty victories in his first attempt. Had David subscribed to the one-prayer creed he could have reduced his psalms to about one-third their present length. Elijah would not have prayed seven times for rain (and incidentally, there would have been no rain, either), our Lord would not have prayed the third time 'saying the same words', nor would Paul have 'besought the Lord thrice' for the removal of his thorn. In fact, if this teaching were true, much wonderful biblical narrative would have to be rewritten, for the Bible has much to say about continued and persistent prayer.

One thing hidden in such teachings as have been mentioned above is unconscious spiritual pride. The Christian who refuses to confess sin on the ground that it is already forgiven is setting himself above prophet and psalmist and all the saints who have left anything on record about themselves from Paul to the present time. These did not hide their sins behind a syllogism, but eagerly and fully confessed them. Perhaps that is why they were such great souls and those who claim to have found a better way are so small.

And one has but to note the smug smile of superiority on the face of the one-prayer Christian to sense that there is a lot of pride behind the smile. While other Christians wrestle with God in an agony of intercession they sit back in humble pride waiting it out. They do not pray because they have already prayed. The devil has no fear of such Christians. He has already won over them, and his technique has been false logic.

Let's use both wings. We'll get further that way.

18

Our Unclaimed Riches

Those spiritual blessings in heavenly places which are ours in Christ may be divided into three classes:

The first is those which come to us immediately upon our believing unto salvation, such as forgiveness, justification, regeneration, sonship to God and baptism into the Body of Christ. In Christ we possess these even before we know that they are ours, such knowledge coming to us later through the study of the Holy Scriptures.

The second class is those riches which are ours by inheritance but which we cannot enjoy in actuality until our Lord returns. These include ultimate mental and moral perfection, the glorification of our bodies, the completion of the restoration of the divine image in our redeemed personalities and the admission into the very presence of God to experience for ever the Beatific Vision. These treasures are as surely ours as if we possessed them now, but it would be useless for us to pray for them while we journey here below. God has made it very clear that they are reserved for the time of the manifestation of the sons of God (Rom 8:18–25).

The third class of blessing consists of spiritual treasures which are ours by blood atonement but which will not come to us unless we make a determined effort to possess them. These are deliverance from the sins of the flesh, victory over self, the constant flow of the Holy Spirit through our personalities, fruitfulness in Christian service, awareness of the presence of God, growth in grace, an increasing consciousness of union with God and an unbroken spirit of worship. These do not come to us automatically nor must we wait to claim them at the day of Christ's coming. They are to us what the Promised Land was to Israel, to be entered into as our faith and courage mount.

To make things clearer let me set forth four propositions touching this heritage of joy which God has set before us:

1. *You will get nothing unless you go after it.* God will not force anything on you. As Joshua fought his way into possession of the Promised Land you also must fight on toward perfection, meeting and defeating whatever enemies would stand in the way to challenge your right of possession. The land will not come to you; you must go to the land and on up into it by the way of self-renunciation and detachment from the world. 'Those who travel on this road,' says John of the Cross, 'will meet many occasions of joys and sufferings, hopes and sorrows, some of which are the result of the spirit of perfection, others of imperfection.'

2. *You may have as much as you insist upon having.* 'Every place that the sole of your foot shall tread upon, that have I given unto you,' said God to Joshua, and this principle runs throughout the entire Bible. The history of Israel is dotted with stories of those who pressed boldly on to claim their possessions; such, for instance, as Caleb who, after the conquest of Canaan, went to Joshua, demanded the mountain Moses had promised him, and got it. Again, when the daughters of Zelophehad stood before Moses and pleaded, 'Give unto us...a possession among the brethren of our father,' their request was granted. Those women received their inheritance, not by the indulgence of

Moses but by the command of God whose promise was involved. When our requests are such as honour God we may ask as largely as we will. The more daring the request the more glory accrues to God when the answer comes.

3. *You will have as little as you are satisfied with.* God giveth to all men liberally, but it would be absurd to think that God's liberality will make a man more godly than he wants to be. The man, for instance, who is satisfied to live a defeated life will never be forced to take victory. The man who is content to follow Christ afar off will never know the radiant wonder of His nearness. The man who is willing to settle for a joyless, barren life will never experience the joy of the Holy Spirit or the deep satisfaction of fruitful living.

It is disheartening to those who care, and surely a great grief to the Spirit, to see how many Christians are content to settle for less than the best. Personally I have for years carried a burden of sorrow as I have moved among evangelical Christians who somewhere in their past have managed to strike a base compromise with their heart's holier longings and have settled down to a lukewarm, mediocre kind of Christianity utterly unworthy of themselves and of the Lord they claim to serve. And such are found everywhere.

4. *You now have as much as you really want.* Every man is as close to God as he wants to be; he is as holy and as full of the Spirit as he wills to be. Our Lord said, 'Blessed are they which do hunger and thirst after righteousness: for they shall be filled.' If there were but one man anywhere on earth who hungered and was not filled the word of Christ would fall to the ground.

Yet we must distinguish wanting from wishing. By 'want' I mean whole-hearted desire. Certainly there are many who wish they were holy or victorious or joyful but are not willing to meet God's conditions to obtain.

That God has placed before His redeemed children a vast world of spiritual treasures and that they refuse or neglect to claim it may easily turn out to be the second greatest tragedy in the history of the moral creation, the first and greatest being the fall of man.

19

Living the God-conscious Life

If God is the Supreme Good then our highest blessedness on earth must lie in knowing Him as perfectly as
possible.

The ultimate end to which redemption leads is the
immediate sight of the ever-blessed Godhead. In our
present state we cannot with our natural eyes look upon
God, for it is written, 'Thou canst not see my face: for
there shall no man see me, and live' (Ex 33:20).

When the work of Christ has been completed in His
people, however, it will be possible, even natural, for
redeemed men to behold their Redeemer. This is stated
plainly by the apostle John: 'But we know that, when he
shall appear, we shall be like him; for we shall see him as
he is' (1 Jn 3:2). And it is also written, 'The throne of
God and of the Lamb shall be in it; and his servants shall
serve him: and they shall see his face' (Rev 22:3, 4).

This rapturous experience has been called the Beatific
Vision and will be the culmination of all possible human
blessedness. It will bring the glorified saint into a state of
perpetual bliss which to taste for even one moment will
banish for ever from his mind every memory of grief or
suffering here below. This will be the portion of all
overcomers. Bernard of Cluny described it this way:

Thou feel'st in mystic rapture,
  O Bride that know'st no guile,
The Prince's sweetest kisses,
  The Prince's loveliest smile;
Unfading lilies, bracelets
  Of living pearl thine own;
The Lamb is ever near thee,
  The Bridegroom thine alone.
The Crown is He to guerdon,
  The Buckler to protect,
And He Himself the Mansion,
  And He the Architect.

It is true that a select company of Christians through the centuries have testified that they were rapt into a state where for varying lengths of time they were able to experience the Beatific Vision at least to some degree while still here in their natural bodies, seeing the ever-blessed one not with their physical eyes but with the eye of the Spirit.

Being myself extremely cautious and slow to accept the unusual, I have tended to back away from this burning bush; but the holy characters of some of those who made such claims, their salty good sense and their sound basic theology along with their devoted service to mankind, have certainly placed them above the faintest suspicion of being fanatics or impostors. I for one must accept their testimony as valid.

I suppose the vast majority of us must wait for the great day of the Lord's coming to realise the full wonder of the vision of God Most High. In the meantime we are, I believe, missing a great measure of radiant glory that is ours by blood-covenant and available to us in this present world if we would but believe it and press on in the way of holiness.

In seeking to know God better we must keep firmly in mind that we need not try to persuade God. He is already persuaded in our favour, not by our prayers but by the generous goodness of His own heart. 'It is God's nature to give Himself to every virtuous soul,' says Meister Eckhart. 'Know then that God is bound to act, to pour Himself out into thee as soon as ever He shall find thee ready.' As nature abhors a vacuum, so the Holy Spirit rushes in to fill the nature that has become empty by separating itself from the world and sin. This is not an unnatural act and need not be an unusual one, for it is in perfect accord with the nature of God. He must act as He does because He is God.

It is hardly possible to over-stress the importance of unceasing inward prayer on the part of the one who would live the God-conscious life. Prayer at stated times is good and right; we will never outgrow the need of it while we remain on earth. But this kind of prayer must be supported and perfected by the habit of constant, unspoken prayer.

But someone may question whether in a world like this it is possible to think of God constantly. Would it not be too great a burden to try to keep God constantly in the focus of our minds while carrying on our normal activities in this noisy and highly complex civilisation? Malaval had the answer to this: 'The wings of the dove do not weigh it down,' he said; 'they carry and support it. And so the thought of God is never a burden; it is a gentle breeze which bears us up, a hand which supports us and raises us, a light which guides us, and a spirit which vivifies us though we do not feel its working.'

We all know how the presence of someone we deeply love lifts our spirits and suffuses us with a radiant sense of peace and well-being. So the one who loves God supremely is lifted into rapture by His conscious presence. 'Then were the disciples glad, when they saw the Lord.'

If only we would stop lamenting and look up. God is here. Christ is risen. The Spirit has been poured out from on high. All this we know as theological truth. It remains for us to turn it into joyous spiritual experience.

And how is this accomplished? There is no new technique; if it is new it is false. The old, old method still works. Conscious fellowship with Christ is by faith, love and obedience. And the humblest believer need not be without these.

20

Believing or Visualising

Unbelief is so prevalent that I do not wish to say anything that might be interpreted as excusing it, but for all our being so slow to believe I still think that sometimes we blame ourselves for unbelief when our trouble is nothing more than inability to visualise.

There are some truths set forth in the Scriptures that place a great strain upon our minds. Divine revelation assures us that certain things are true which imagination will simply not grasp. We believe them but we cannot see them in the mind's eye.

It may be pointed out here that the ease with which we grasp a truth is sure to be in exact proportion to its externality as distinguished from its internality. Biblical history, for instance, because it is all objective and external, is no problem to belief. We are sure we believe whatever is written about Moses or David or Peter because we have no trouble 'seeing' it taking place, while such truths as regeneration or the divine indwelling cannot be visualised and so are more difficult for us to handle. This we should recognise as psychological, not spiritual, and stop chiding ourselves for something we have not done.

As I have said many times before, we cannot be right unless we think right, and to think right we must distinguish believing from visualising. The two are not the same. One is moral and the other mental. Unwillingness to believe proves that men love darkness rather than light, while inability to visualise indicates no more than lack of imagination, something that will not be held against us at the judgement seat of Christ.

The ability to visualise is found among vigorous-minded persons, whatever their moral or spiritual condition may be. A man with no faith in God or Christ may nevertheless have a keen imagination that enables him to picture inwardly anything he hears described. He gets on very well without charts and illustrations since he can create an inward image as clear as a photograph. Another man who believes the Word of God implicitly and proves it by a life of obedience and charity may yet find it very hard to envisage the things he believes. Such a man is likely to blame himself for what he feels is unbelief.

The wise Christian will not let his assurance depend upon his powers of imagination. Personally I find it difficult to picture the resurrection and the future life. I believe without reservation everything that is written in the Scriptures about this, and I can affirm with the whole family of God,

> *I believe in the Holy Ghost;*
> *The holy catholic Church;*
> *The communion of saints;*
> *The forgiveness of sins;*
> *The resurrection of the body;*
> *And the life everlasting.*

Still I obtain little satisfaction from the effort to picture the resurrection and the glorified state. I have pored over the Book of Revelation without receiving much help in my attempt to visualise the life to come. I have meditated lovingly upon Bernard's sweet hymn of heaven, 'The Celestial Country', and my heart has some-times been raised to near ecstasy by the scenes depicted there; yet when I try to imagine myself in that place my mind faints with the effort. I believe with unshakable confidence that our Lord has gone to prepare us a place and that He will come to take us unto Himself, but I cannot form a mental image of it.

Undoubtedly Bernard himself, for all his brilliant imagination and his insight into the Scriptures, sometimes found it hard to believe that he himself would actually walk within the heavenly mansions and gaze with his own eyes upon the Beatific Vision. At first I wanted to blame him a little for what seemed a doubt when he wrote,

> *O sweet and blessed country,*
> *Shall I ever see thy face?*
> *O sweet and blessed country,*
> *Shall I ever win thy grace?*
> *I have the hope within me*
> *To comfort and to bless!*
> *Shall I ever win the prize itself?*
> *O tell me, tell me, Yes!*

Then I read the triumphant answer he gave to his own question and I understood:

> *Exult, O dust and ashes!*
> *The Lord shall be thy part;*
> *His only, His for ever,*
> *Thou shalt be, and thou art!*

True faith is not the intellectual ability to visualise unseen things to the satisfaction of our imperfect minds; it is rather the moral power to trust Christ. To be contented and unafraid when going on a journey with his father the child need not be able to imagine events; he need but know the father. Our earthly lives are one shining web of golden mystery which we experience without understanding, how much more our life in the Spirit. Jesus Christ is our all in all. We need but trust Him and He will take care of the rest.

Possibly it is because of my own innate dullness that I have found such deep satisfaction in these words of the prophet: 'I will bring the blind by a way that they knew not; I will lead them in paths that they have not known: I will make darkness light before them, and crooked things straight. These things will I do unto them, and not forsake them' (Isa 42:16). God has not failed me in this world; I can trust Him for the world to come.

21

The Christian Life Is Not Easy

As we move farther on and mount higher up in the Christian life we may expect to encounter greater difficulties in the way and meet increased hostility from the enemy of our souls. Though this is seldom presented to Christians as a fact of life it is a very solid fact indeed as every experienced Christian knows, and one we shall learn how to handle or stumble over to our own undoing.

Satan hates the true Christian for several reasons. One is that God loves him, and whatever is loved by God is sure to be hated by the devil. Another is that the Christian, being a child of God, bears a family resemblance to the Father and to the household of faith. Satan's ancient jealousy has not abated nor his hatred for God diminished in the slightest. Whatever reminds him of God is without other reason the object of his malignant hate.

A third reason is that a true Christian is a former slave who has escaped from the galley, and Satan cannot forgive him for this affront. A fourth reason is that a praying Christian is a constant threat to the stability of Satan's government. The Christian is a holy rebel loose in the world with access to the throne of God. Satan never knows from what direction the danger will come. Who knows when another Elijah will arise, or another

Daniel? or a Luther or a Booth? Who knows when an Edwards or a Finney may go in and liberate a whole town or countryside by the preaching of the Word and prayer? Such a danger is too great to tolerate, so Satan gets to the new convert as early as possible to prevent his becoming too formidable a foe.

The new believer thus becomes at once a principal target for the fiery darts of the devil. Satan knows that the best way to be rid of a soldier is to destroy him before he becomes a man. The young Moses must not be allowed to grow into a liberator to set a nation free. The baby Jesus dare not be permitted to become a man to die for the sins of the world. The new Christian must be destroyed early, or at least he must have his growth stunted so that he will be no real problem later.

Now I do not think that Satan much cares to destroy us Christians physically. The soldier dead in battle who died performing some deed of heroism is not a great loss to the army but may rather be an object of pride to his country. On the other hand the soldier who cannot or will not fight but runs away at the sound of the first enemy gun is a shame to his family and a disgrace to his nation. So a Christian who dies in the faith represents no irreparable loss to the forces of righteousness on earth and certainly no victory for the devil. But when whole regiments of professed believers are too timid to fight and too smug to be ashamed, surely it must bring an astringent smile to the face of the enemy; and it should bring a blush to the cheeks of the whole Church of Christ.

The devil's master strategy for us Christians then is not to kill us physically (though there may be some special situations where physical death fits into his plan better), but to destroy our power to wage spiritual warfare. And how well he has succeeded. The average Christian these days is a harmless enough thing. God knows. He is a child wearing with considerable self-consciousness the harness of the warrior; he is a sick eaglet that can never mount up with wings; he is a spent pilgrim who has given up the journey and sits with a waxy smile trying to get what pleasure he can from sniffing the wilted flowers he has plucked by the way.

Such as these have been reached. Satan has got to them early. By means of false teaching or inadequate teaching, or the huge discouragement that comes from the example of a decadent church, he has succeeded in weakening their resolution, neutralising their convictions and taming their original urge to do exploits; now they are little more than statistics that contribute financially to the upkeep of the religious institution. And how many a pastor is content to act as a patient, smiling curator of a church full (or a quarter full) of such blessed spiritual museum pieces.

If Satan opposes the new convert he opposes still more bitterly the Christian who is pressing on toward a higher life in Christ. The Spirit-filled life is not, as many suppose, a life of peace and quiet pleasure. It is likely to be something quite the opposite.

Viewed one way it is a pilgrimage through a robber-infested forest; viewed another, it is a grim warfare with the devil. Always there is struggle, and sometimes there is a pitched battle with our own nature where the lines are so confused that it is all but impossible to locate the enemy or to tell which impulse is of the Spirit and which of the flesh.

There is complete victory for us if we will but take the way of the triumphant Christ, but that is not what we are considering now. My point here is that if we want to escape the struggle we have but to draw back and accept the currently accepted low-keyed Christian life as the normal one. That is all Satan wants. That will ground our power, stunt our growth and render us harmless to the kingdom of darkness.

Compromise will take the pressure off. Satan will not bother a man who has quit fighting. But the cost of quitting will be a life of peaceful stagnation. We sons of eternity just cannot afford such a thing.

22

Affirmation and Denial

The notion that we enter the Christian life by an act of acceptance is true, but that is not all the truth. There is much more to it than that. Christianity involves an acceptance and a repudiation, an affirmation and a denial. And this not only at the moment of conversion but continually thereafter day by day in all the battle of life till the great conflict is over and the Christian is home from the wars.

To live a life wholly positive is, fortunately, impossible. Were any man able to do such a thing it could be only for a moment. Living positively would be like inhaling continuously without exhaling. Aside from its being impossible, it would be fatal. Exhalation is as necessary to life as inhalation.

To accept Christ it is necessary that we reject whatever is contrary to Him. This is a fact often overlooked by eager evangelists bent on getting results. Like the salesman who talks up the good points of his product and conceals its disadvantages, the badly informed soul-winner stresses the positive side of things at the expense of the negative.

Let us not be shocked by the suggestion that there are disadvantages to the life in Christ. There most certainly are. Abel was murdered, Joseph was sold into slavery,

Daniel was thrown into the den of lions, Stephen was stoned to death, Paul was beheaded, and a noble army of martyrs was put to death by various painful methods all down the long centuries. And where the hostility did not lead to such violence (and mostly it did not and does not) the sons of this world nevertheless managed to make it tough for the children of God in a thousand cruel ways. Everyone who has lived for Christ in a Christless world has suffered some losses and endured some pains that he could have avoided by the simple expedient of laying down his cross.

However, the pains are short and the losses inconsequential compared with the glory that will follow, 'for our light affliction, which is but for a moment, worketh for us a far more exceeding and eternal weight of glory' (2 Cor 4:17). But while we are here among men with our sensitive hearts exposed to the chilly blasts of the unbelieving and uncomprehending world it is imperative that we take a realistic view of things and learn how to deal with disadvantages. And it is important that we tell the whole truth to those we are endeavouring to win.

The astute Mark Twain once pointed out that some churches actually fail to gain members because they make the way too easy, and conversely the church that is hard to get into is the one that is likely to prosper numerically. The experienced missionary knows that the book or Scripture portion that is given away free will be less valued by the receiver than if a small price had been paid for it. And the higher the price the more precious the possession.

Our Lord called men to follow Him but He never made the way look easy. Indeed one gets the distinct impression that He made it appear extremely hard. Sometimes He said things to disciples or prospective disciples that we today discreetly avoid repeating when we are trying to win men to Him. What present-day evangelist would have the courage to tell an inquirer, 'If any man will come after me, let him deny himself, and take up his cross, and follow me. For whosoever will save his life shall lose it: but whosoever will lose his life for my sake, the same shall save it' (Lk 9:23, 24)? And do not we do some tall explaining when someone asks us what Jesus meant when He said, 'Think not that I am come to send peace on earth: I came not to send peace, but a sword. For I am come to set a man at variance against his father, and the daughter against her mother, and the daughter in law against her mother in law' (Matt 10:34, 35)? That kind of rugged, sinewy Christianity is left for an occasional missionary or for some believer behind one of the various curtains in the world. The masses of professed Christians simply do not have the moral muscle to enable them to take a path so downright and final as this.

The contemporary moral climate does not favour a faith as tough and fibrous as that taught by our Lord and His apostles. The delicate, brittle saints being produced in our religious hothouses today are hardly to be compared with the committed, expendable believers who once gave their witness among men. And the fault lies with our leaders. They are too timid to tell the people all the truth. They are now asking men to give to God that which costs them nothing.

Our churches these days are filled (or one-quarter filled) with a soft breed of Christian that must be fed on a diet of harmless fun to keep them interested. About theology they know little. Scarcely any of them have read even one of the great Christian classics, but most of them are familiar with religious fiction and spine-tingling films. No wonder their moral and spiritual constitution is so frail. Such can only be called weak adherents of a faith they never really understood.

When will Christians learn that to love righteousness it is necessary to hate sin? that to accept Christ it is necessary to reject self? that to follow the good way we must flee from evil? that a friend of the world is an enemy of God? that God allows no twilight zone between two altogethers where the fearful and the doubting may take refuge at once from hell to come and the rigours of present discipline?

23

The Giver and the Taker

'God's Gifts,' said Meister Eckhart, 'are meted out according to the taker, not according to the giver.' Did we enjoy God's gifts according to the giver there would be no spiritual poverty among us, for surely there is no lack in God.

Were I offered my choice to receive spiritual benefits that accord with my ability to ask or with God's willingness to give, I would not hesitate a moment. By all means let me fall into the hands of God rather than into the hands of men, or even into my own hands. I cannot want a benefit as eagerly as God wants to give it to me. My asking is likely to be limited by many human factors, and my boldest request is sure to be small. God's willingness to give is unlimited and His ability to perform what He wills is boundless.

When the Queen of Sheba visited King Solomon she received two kinds of treasures. The first was according to her asking: 'King Solomon gave unto the queen of Sheba all her desire, whatsoever she asked.' It is not possible to tell how seriously she may have deprived herself by her limited asking. Modesty, pride, doubt, timidity—all these or any of them might have lurked in her heart and restrained her asking. We have but to look in our own hearts to discover how she acted. She too was human.

But King Solomon would display his magnanimity, so
he gave her all she asked 'beside that which Solomon
gave her of his royal bounty'. So she departed, rich both
from her own asking and from Solomon's unsolicited
giving. From what we know of King Solomon is it not
reasonable to suppose that his voluntary bounty went far
beyond her highest expectation? She had brought him
gifts of gold and precious stones and spices. Surely he
more than matched her generosity.

Since God is infinite, whatever He is must be infinite
also; that is, it must be without any actual or conceivable
limits. The moment we allow ourselves to think of God
as having limits, the one of whom we are thinking is not
God but someone or something less than and different
from Him. To think rightly of God we must conceive of
Him as being altogether boundless in His goodness,
mercy, love, grace, and in whatever else we may properly attribute to the Deity.

It is not enough that we acknowledge God's infinite
resources; we must believe also that He is infinitely
generous to bestow them. The first is not too great a
strain on our faith. Even the deist will admit that the
Most High God, possessor of heaven and earth, must be
rich beyond the power of man to conceive. But to
believe that God is a giver as well as a possessor takes an
advanced faith and presupposes that there has been a
divine revelation to that effect which gives validity to our
expectations. Which indeed there has been. We call this
revelation the Bible.

Believing all this, why are we Christians so poverty-
stricken? I think it is because we have not learned that
God's gifts are meted out according to the taker, not
according to the giver. Though almighty and all-wise,
God yet cannot pour a great gift into a small receptacle.

To receive in a measure more in keeping with God's
liberality five things are necessary. The first is *faith*. We
must be convinced that God is kind, generous, good-
hearted and ready to bestow His blessings upon His

people with the bounty of a king. To have faith we must immerse ourselves in the Scriptures. And faith must be exercised if it is to be effective. Faith, like a muscle, grows by stretching.

The second is *capacity*. That we differ from each other in spiritual capacity is too evident to need proof; but the reason is a great mystery and lies too deep for our understanding, certainly too deep for discussion here. It is enough to say that whatever his capacity each man can increase it if he will. The human soul is not a hard-baked vessel with a fixed size; it is a living thing capable of growth and expansion as it interacts with the gracious actions of the Holy Spirit.

The third is *receptivity*, and one factor always present in receptivity is interest. It is virtually impossible to receive into our minds anything in which we have no interest. A man of ordinary mind may go on to do marvels in a given field if he has keen enough interest in it, and leave behind many men of finer minds who lack the necessary interest. Sometimes one interest may crowd out another. I wonder how many potential Rubinsteins or Heifetzes may have got lost in obscurity simply because they could not as boys bring themselves to practice when a football game was in progress nearby. So worldly interests often crowd out heavenly ones and spiritual receptivity is destroyed as a result.

The fourth is *responsibility*. The gifts of God are given to us to use. When they are not used they atrophy. The story of the ten talents should be a warning to all of us. When writing about the gifts of the Spirit the apostle Paul explained that these manifestations of the Spirit were given to everyone for the profit of all. Selfish attitudes toward the blessings of God can destroy their usefulness. We have a serious responsibility in this matter.

The fifth is *gratitude*. It is impossible to be too thankful to God, but it might be good to try it. Our wise Father does not usually give a second gift until we properly praise Him for the first.

24

There Is No Substitute for Theology

We being what we are and all things else being what they are, the most important and profitable study any of us can engage in is without question the study of theology.

That theology probably receives less attention than any other subject tells us nothing about its importance or lack of it. It indicates rather that men are still hiding from the presence of God among the trees of the garden and feel acutely uncomfortable when the matter of their relation to God is brought up. They sense their deep alienation from God and only manage to live at peace with themselves by forgetting that they are not at peace with God.

If there were no God things would be quite otherwise with us. Were there no one to whom we must finally render up account, at least one big load would be gone from our minds. We would only need to live within the law, not too hard a task in most countries, and there would be nothing to fear. But if God indeed created the earth and placed man upon it in a state of moral probation, then the heavy obligation lies upon us to learn the will of God and do it.

It has always seemed to me completely inconsistent that existentialism should deny the existence of God and then proceed to use the language of theism to persuade men to live right. The French writer, Jean-Paul Sartre, for instance, states frankly that he represents atheistic existentialism. 'If God does not exist,' he says, 'we find no values or commands to turn to which legitimise our conduct. So in the bright realm of values, we have no excuse behind us, nor justification before us. We are all alone, with no excuses.' Yet in the next paragraph he states bluntly, 'Man is responsible for his passion,' and further on, 'A coward is responsible for his cowardice.' And such considerations as these, he says, fill the existentialist with 'anguish, forlornness and despair.'

It seems to me that such reasoning must assume the truth of everything it seeks to deny. If there were no God there could be no such word as 'responsible'. No criminal need fear a judge who does not exist; nor would he need to worry about breaking a law that had not been passed. It is the knowledge that the law and the judge do in fact exist that strikes fear to the law-breaker's heart. There is someone to whom he is accountable; otherwise the concept of responsibility could have no meaning.

It is precisely because God *is,* and because man is made in His image and is accountable to Him, that theology is so critically important. Christian revelation alone has the answer to life's unanswered questions about God and human destiny. To let these authoritative answers lie neglected while we search everywhere else for answers and find none is, it seems to me, nothing less than folly.

No motorist would be excused if he neglected to consult his road map and tried instead to find his way across the country by looking for moss on logs, or by observing the flight of wild bees or watching the movements of the heavenly bodies. If there *were* no map a man *might* find his way by the stars; but for a traveller trying to get home the stars would be a poor substitute for a map.

Without a map the Greeks did an admirable piece of navigating; but the Hebrews possessed the map and so had no need of human philosophy. As one not wholly unacquainted with Greek thought I state it is my belief that but one of Isaiah's eloquent chapters or David's inspired psalms contains more real help for mankind than all the output of the finest minds of Greece during the centuries of her glory.

The present neglect of the inspired Scriptures by civilised man is a shame and a scandal; for those same Scriptures tell him all he wants to know, or should want to know, about God, his own soul and human destiny. It is ironic that men will spend vast amounts both of time and of money in an effort to uncover the secrets of their past when their own future is all that should really matter to them.

No man is responsible for his ancestors; and the only past he must account for is the relatively short one he himself has lived here on earth. To learn how I can escape the guilt of sins committed in my brief yesterdays, how I can live free from sin today and enter at last into the blessed presence of God in a happy tomorrow—that is more important to me than anything that can be discovered by the anthropologist. It appears to me to be a strange perversion of interest to gaze backward at the dust when we are equipped to look upward at the glory.

Whatever keeps me from the Bible is my enemy, however harmless it may appear to be. Whatever engages my attention when I should be meditating on God and things eternal does injury to my soul. Let the cares of life crowd out the Scriptures from my mind and I have suffered loss where I can least afford it. Let me accept anything else instead of the Scriptures and I have been cheated and robbed to my eternal confusion.

The secret of life is theological and the key to heaven as well. We learn with difficulty, forget easily and suffer many distractions. Therefore we should set our hearts to study theology. We should preach it from our pulpits, sing it in our hymns, teach it to our children and make it the subject of conversation when we meet with Christian friends.

25

The Increasing Knowledge of God

Without doubt the greatest need of the human personality is to experience God Himself. This is because of who God is and who and what man is.

God is the essence of intelligent, self-conscious life and man is created in His image. God is love, and man is made for God. God and man exist for each other and neither is satisfied without the other. Though God is self-sufficient He has sovereignly willed to have communion with the being He made in honour next to Himself, and He takes every means to secure this communion short of coercion, which would be a violation of man's free will. Were God to override our wills He would be forcing Himself upon us and by so doing would make us a little less than human and so a little less than the being He made for Himself.

That first picture of God and man at the time of the creation shows them in close and open-hearted communion. Adam listens while God explains how it is to be with him in his Eden home and lays down a few easy rules for his life on the earth. The whole scene is restful, relaxed and altogether beautiful.

But the communion did not last. Adam's very likeness to God, viz., his freedom to choose, permitted him, though it did not compel him, to make a choice contrary to the will of God. So sin entered and the wondrous fellowship was broken.

Seen from our human standpoint redemption must rank first among all the acts of God. No other achievement of the Godhead required such vast and precise knowledge, such perfection of wisdom or such fullness of moral power. To bring man into communion with Himself God must deal effectively with the whole matter of justice and righteousness; He must dispose of sin, reconcile an enemy and make a rebel willingly obedient. And this He must do without compromising His holiness or coercing the race He would save.

How two wills set in opposition to each other, and both free, could be harmonised was God's problem and His alone; and with infinite wisdom and power He solved it through the redemptive work of Jesus Christ our Lord. Because Christ is God and man He can properly represent each before the other. He is the Arbitrator who can stand between the alienated man and the offended God and lay His hand upon them both. 'For there is one God, and one mediator between God and men, the man Christ Jesus' (1 Tim 2:5).

All this is such a familiar part of evangelical theology that it may safely be assumed that the majority of my readers know it already. That is, they know it theoretically, but the experiential aspect of the truth is not so well known. Indeed large numbers of supposedly sound Christian believers know nothing at all about personal communion with God; and there lies one of the greatest weaknesses of present-day Christianity.

The experiential knowledge of God is eternal life (John 17:3), and increased knowledge results in a correspondingly larger and fuller life. So rich a treasure is this inward knowledge of God that every other treasure is as nothing compared with it. We may count all things of no value and sacrifice them freely if we may thereby gain a more perfect knowledge of God through Jesus Christ our Lord. This was Paul's testimony (Phil 3:7–14) and it has been the testimony of all great Christian souls who have followed Christ from Paul's day to ours.

To know God it is necessary that we be like God to some degree, for things wholly dissimilar cannot agree and beings wholly unlike can never have communion with each other. It is necessary therefore that we use every means of grace to bring our souls into harmony with the character of God.

'Thou art to know that thy soul is the centre, habitation, and kingdom of God,' says Molinos. 'That therefore, to the end the sovereign King may rest on that throne, thou oughtest to take pains to keep thy soul pure, quiet, void and peaceable; pure from guilt and defects; quiet from fears; void of affections, desires and thoughts; and peaceable in temptation and tribulation. Thou oughtest always then to keep thine heart in peace, that thou mayest keep pure that temple of God, and with a right and pure intention thou art to work, pray, obey, and suffer, without being in the least disturbed, whatever it pleases the Lord to send unto thee.'

To enjoy this growing knowledge of God will require that we go beyond the goals so casually set by modern evangelicals. We must fix our hearts on God and purposefully aim to rise above the dead level and average of current Christianity.

If we do this Satan will surely tempt us by accusing us of spiritual pride and our friends will warn us to beware of being 'holier than thou'. But as the land of promise had to be taken by storm against the determined opposition of the enemy, so we must capture new spiritual heights over the sour and violent protests of the devil.

As we move farther up into the knowledge of Christ we open new areas of our beings to attack, but what of it? Remember that spiritual complacency is more deadly than anything the devil can bring against us in our upward struggle. If we sit still to escape temptation, then we are being tempted worse than before and gaining nothing by it.

'Ye have dwelt long enough in this mount: ... Behold, I have set the land before you: go in and possess the land' (Dt 1:6, 8).

26

Resisting the Enemy

Someday the church can relax her guard, call her watchmen down from the wall and live in safety and peace; but not yet, not yet.

All that is good in the world stands as a target for all that is evil and manages to stay alive only by constant watchfulness and the providential protection of Almighty God. As a man or a nation may be in deepest trouble when unaware of any trouble at all and in gravest danger when ignorant that any danger exists, so the church may be in greatest peril by not recognising the presence of peril or the source from which it comes.

The church at Laodicea has stood for nineteen hundred years as a serious warning to the whole church of Christ to be most watchful when no enemy is in sight and to remain poor in spirit when earthly wealth increases, yet we appear to have learned nothing from her. We expound the seven letters to the churches of Asia and then return to our own company to live like the Laodicean church. There is in us a bent to backsliding that is all but impossible to cure.

The healthiest man has enough lethal bacteria in him to kill him within twenty-four hours except for one thing–the amazing power of the human organism to resist bacterial attack. Every mortal body must fight its internal enemies day and night. Once it surrenders its hours are numbered. Quite literally it must fight or die.

The reason for this is that the human race inhabits a fallen world which is in many ways hostile to it. Nature as well as man is fallen; and as sin is normal human powers gone astray, so disease results from microscopic creatures once meant to be useful to men but now out of hand and perverted. To live, the body must resist these invisible enemies successfully, and considering our high vulnerability and the number of our enemies it is wonderful that any of us manages to live beyond his childhood.

The church lives in a hostile world. Within and around her are enemies that not only could destroy her, but are meant to and will unless she resists force with yet greater force. The Christian would collapse from sheer external pressure were there not within him a counter-pressure sufficiently great to prevent it. The power of the Holy Spirit is, therefore, not optional but necessary. Without it the children of God simply cannot live the life of heaven on earth. The hindrances are too many and too effective.

A church is a living organism and is subject to attack from such enemies as prey on living things. Yet the figure of the human body to stand for the church is not adequate, for the life of the body is non-intelligent, whereas the church is composed of moral beings having intelligence to recognise their enemies and a will to enable them to resist. The human body can fight its enemies even while it is asleep, but the church cannot. She must be awake and determined or she cannot win.

One enemy we must resist is *unbelief*. The temptation is strong to reject what we cannot explain, or at least to withhold belief till we have investigated further. This attitude is proper, even commendable, for the scientist, but wholly wrong for the Christian. Here is the reason:

The faith of the Christian rests down squarely upon the man Christ Jesus who declares that He is both God and Lord. This claim must be received by pure faith or rejected outright; it can never be proved by investigation. That is why Christ's appeal is directed to faith alone. The believer thinks, it is true; but he thinks because he believes, not in order that he may. Faith secures from the indwelling Spirit confirmation exquisitely perfect, but only after it is there without other support than Christ Himself.

Another enemy is *complacency*. 'Woe to them that are at ease in Zion.' The contented Christian is not in danger of attack, he has already been attacked. He is sick and does not know it. To escape this we must stir up the gift of God which is in us. We must declare war on contentment and press toward the mark for the prize of the high calling of God in Christ Jesus.

Again, there is *self-righteousness*. The temptation to feel morally pleased with ourselves will be all the greater as our lives become better. The only sure defence against this is to cultivate a quiet state of continual penitence. A sweet but sobering memory of our past guilt and a knowledge of our present imperfections are not incompatible with the joy of the Lord; and they are of inestimable aid in resisting the enemy.

The fear of man brings a snare, said the prophet, and this enemy, too, must be defeated. Our whole modern world is geared to destroy individual independence and bring all of us into conformity to all the rest of us. Any deviation from the pattern, whatever that pattern may be at the time, will not be forgiven by society, and since the Christian must deviate radically from the world he naturally comes in for the world's displeasure. If he surrenders to fear he has been conquered, and he dare not let this happen.

Other enemies may be identified, such as *love of luxury, secret sympathy with the world, self-confidence, pride* and *unholy thoughts*. These we must resist with every power within us, looking unto Jesus, the author and finisher of our faith.

27

Spiritual Things Must Be Spiritually Discerned

They who think on heavenly things are forced by their psychological structure to use mental raw material borrowed from the earth. And this is certain to show up in their thinking.

Even the Bible, to be understood by its readers, must condescend to tell of eternal things in the language of time. It must explain the celestial by means of the mundane. So we find in the Scriptures birds and kings and sheep and soldiers acting as interpreters for Almighty God. Grapes and lilies, gold and stubble, corn and cattle, rain and stars all are used by the Holy Spirit to carry our minds across the vast chasm that separates the spiritual from the material.

Doubtless the constant use of figures drawn from our familiar world to express religious ideas leaves a residuum at the bottom of our minds which in some measure gives colour if not form to our theology. We struggle to understand spiritual things by comparing them to natural ones; then little by little those natural things become identified with the spiritual completely and the spiritual suffers greatly as a consequence.

One task of the illuminated Christian teacher is to internalise worship and raise the religious concepts of church people above the figures and allegories that enabled them to grasp those concepts in the first place. The figure is the box in which the shining jewel is carried; but it is surprisingly easy to mistake the box for the jewel and look for nothing more.

Christianity is the religion of the heart. It searches for and finds the man under his wrappings. The gospel reaches the man far in where there is nothing to distinguish him from any other man. Whether he is dark or red or white matters not at all; whether he is a Stone Age aborigine in a grass hut or a civilised white man in an air-conditioned office he is the same man underneath, and it is for that man that the Spirit keeps up His persistent search.

It would appear obvious enough once we think of it that the image of natural objects treasured in the mind tends to impede the flight of our souls upward into God. Illustrations which, by their very definition, should let in light, if used often and objectified by the artist's brush, become opaque at last and actually shut out the light they were intended to admit.

A familiar example may help me to make my point. The psalmist David, in the most beautiful hymn in the world, teaches us to think of Christ as our Shepherd. The Lord Jesus carried the idea further and talked tenderly of His sheep and of Himself as the Shepherd who should lay down His life for them. The artists took up the idea and depicted Christ as a real shepherd and their work has become so fixed in the minds of Christians that when our Lord returns many of them will be secretly disappointed if He is not carrying a crook in His hand and a woolly lamb under His arm.

In this instance what is intended to assist our understanding, to lift our imagination, to put poetry and music into our hearts, has by our blindness become instead a positive hindrance to our knowledge of Christ. Worse, it has given us not only an inadequate but an erroneous picture of Him. We try to visualise Him and the only image that projects onto the screen is that of an idealised shepherd of the Near East, an image which I am certain Paul and John would never recognise. Paul declared that he knew Christ after the flesh no more, and the same John who had recorded the words of Christ concerning the sheep and the shepherd, when he saw Him as He now is fell at His feet as dead.

Always the Church has been tempted to think of God by the use of images and forms, and always when she has so done she has fallen into externalism and spiritual decay. Some of the greatest books apart from the inspired Scriptures have been written to call the Church back to a purer view of God. Miguel de Molinos, in his *Spiritual Guide,* insists that prayer is 'an ascent or elevation of the mind to God'. 'God is above all creatures,' he says further 'and the soul cannot see Him nor converse with Him if she raise not herself above them all.'

The anonymous author of *The Cloud of Unknowing* says, 'Look the loath to think on aught but Himself. So that naught work in thy wit or in thy will, but only Himself. And do that in thee is to forget all creatures that God ever made and the works of them...let them be and take no heed of them. This is the work that most pleaseth God.'

I think it may be said with a fair degree of accuracy that all the great devotional theologians of the centuries taught the futility of trying to visualise the Godhead. Molinos warned against every effort of the intellect to image God forth. 'She ought to go forward with her love,' he says of the Christian's soul, 'leaving all her understanding behind. Let her love God as He is and not as her understanding says He is, and pictures Him.'

The teaching of the New Testament is that God and spiritual things can be known finally only by a direct work of God within the soul. However theological knowledge may be aided by figures and analogies, the pure understanding of God must be by personal spiritual awareness. The Holy Spirit is indispensable (see Jn 14:1– 16:33 and 1 Cor 1:18–2:16).

28

To Be Understood, Truth Must Be Lived

For a long time I have believed that truth, to be understood, must be lived; that Bible doctrine is wholly ineffective until it has been digested and assimilated by the total life. I have held this to be an important element in the preaching of the Old Testament prophets, and I have felt it to be near to the heart of the moral teaching of our Lord Jesus Christ. I admit that this belief has made me a little lonely, for not many of my Christian brethren share it with me. While I have not heard anyone deny the truth outright, few have seen fit to teach it with anything approaching emphasis. And by silence a man will reveal his beliefs as surely as by argument.

This is one of those truths which at first may appear dull and colourless, but far from being tame or weak, this truth is of tremendous importance to all of us. While not to my knowledge formulated as a tenet in the creed of any church or school of religious thought, it nevertheless stands as a great divide to separate those who think rightly about the faith of Christ from those who think carelessly about it.

The essence of my belief is that there is a difference, a vast difference, between fact and truth. Truth in the Scriptures is more than a fact. A fact may be detached, impersonal, cold and totally dissociated from life. Truth on the other hand, is warm, living and spiritual. A theological fact may be held in the mind for a lifetime without its having any positive effect upon the moral character; but truth is creative, saving, transforming, and it always changes the one who receives it into a humbler and holier man.

At what point, then, does a theological fact become for the one who holds it a life-giving truth? *At the point where obedience begins*. When faith gains the consent of the will to make an irrevocable committal to Christ as Lord, truth begins its saving, illuminating work; and not one moment before.

In His conflict with the religious textualists of His day our Lord often uttered short statements that serve as keys to unlock vast and precious storehouses of truth. In the Gospel according to John these may be found in something amounting to profusion. One such is found in John 7: 'If any man will do his will, he shall know of the doctrine, whether it be of God, or whether I speak of myself' (verse 17). A. T. Robertson, in his *Word Pictures in the New Testament*, explains 'he shall know' as being 'experimental knowledge from willingness to do God's will'. Then he quotes Westcott: 'If there be no sympathy there can be no understanding.'

Obviously these words of Christ were understood by the great British biblical scholar Westcott and the brilliant American expositor Robertson as teaching that truth can be understood only by the mind that has surrendered to it. The average evangelical Bible teacher today finds such a radical interpretation too revolutionary to be comfortable and so just ignores it.

We must be willing to obey if we would know the true inner meaning of the teachings of Christ and the apostles. I believe this view prevailed in every revival that ever came to the church during her long history. Indeed a revived church may be distinguished from a dead one by the attitude of its members toward the truth. The dead church holds to the shell of truth without surrendering the will to it, while the church that wills to do God's will is immediately blessed with a visitation of spiritual powers.

Theological facts are like the altar of Elijah on Carmel before the fire came, correct, properly laid out, but altogether cold. When the heart makes the ultimate surrender, the fire falls and true facts are transmuted into spiritual truth that transforms, enlightens, sanctifies. The church or the individual that is Bible taught without being Spirit taught (and there are many of them) has simply failed to see that truth lies deeper than the theological statement of it.

Truth cannot aid us until we become participators in it. We only possess what we experience. St. Gregory of Sinai, who lived in the fourteenth century, taught that understanding and participation were inseparable in the spiritual life. 'He who seeks to understand commandments without fulfilling commandments, and to acquire such understanding through learning and reading, is like a man who takes a shadow for truth. For the understanding of truth is given to those who have become participants in truth (who have tasted it through living). Those who are not participants in truth and are not initiated therein, when they seek this understanding, draw it from a distorted wisdom. Of such men the apostle says "the natural man receiveth not the things of the Spirit", even though they boast of their knowledge of truth.'

Here is a simple but neglected doctrine that should be restored to its rightful place in the thinking and teaching of the church. It would work wonders.

29

The Sanctification of Our Minds

Thinking is a kind of living. To think and to be aware that we think is to be conscious; life without consciousness is but a shadow of life, having no meaning and being of no value to the individual. Our thoughts are the product of our thinking, and since these are of such vast importance to us it is imperative that we learn how to think rightly.

I am not concerned here with that kind of profound cerebration known as 'heavy thinking'. Few of us have the intellectual equipment to enable us, or the will power to compel us, to engage in such heroic mental exercise. I am dealing here with that kind of thinking done by every normal person every waking moment from birth to death.

After all, it is not our heavy thinking that shapes our characters, but the quiet attention of the mind to the surrounding world day after day throughout our lives. Men are influenced more by their common, everyday thinking than by any rare intellectual feat such as writing a great poem or painting a famous picture. Feats of thinking may create reputation, but habits of thinking create character. The incredible mental accomplishments of an Einstein, for instance, had almost nothing to do with the kind of human being he was; the constant, undramatic, moment-by-moment interplay of his mind with his environment, on the other hand, had almost everything to do with it.

We all live in two environments, the one being the world around us, the other our thoughts about that world. The larger world cannot affect us directly; it must be mediated to us by our thoughts, and will be to us at last only what we allow it to be.

Three men walking side by side may yet be inhabiting three different worlds. Imagine a poet, a naturalist and a lumberjack travelling together through a forest. The poet's mind races back over the centuries to the time when the mighty trees now towering above him were but beginning to appear as tiny green shoots out of the grey earth. He dreams of the mighty of the world who then wore crowns and swayed empires, but who have long ago passed from this earthly scene and been forgotten by everyone but a few historians.

The naturalist's world is smaller and more detailed. He hears the sweet, hardly audible bird song that floats among the branches and seeks to discover the hidden singer; he knows what kind of moss it is that clings to the base of the centuries-old trees; he sees what the others miss, the fresh claw marks on the bark of a tree, and knows that a bear has recently passed that way.

The lumberjack's world is smaller still. He is concerned neither with history nor nature but with lumber. He judges the diameter and height of the tree, and by quick calculation determines how much it will bring on the market. His world is the dull world of commerce. He sees nothing beyond it.

It is obvious that one external world has been turned into three internal worlds by the thinking of the three men. External things and events are the raw material only; the finished product is whatever the mind makes of these. Judas Iscariot and John the Beloved lived in the same world, but how differently they interpreted it. The same may be said of Cain and Abel, Esau and Jacob,

Saul and David. From these we learn that circumstances do not make men; it is their reaction to circumstances that determines what kind of men they will be.

What then can we Christians do? The answer is, 'Let this mind be in you, which was also in Christ Jesus.' 'Know ye not your own selves, how that Jesus Christ is in you, except ye be reprobates?' The mental stuff of the Christian can be and should be modified and conditioned by the Spirit of Christ which indwells his nature. God wills that we think His thoughts after Him. The Spirit-filled, prayerful Christian actually possesses the mind of Christ, so that his reactions to the external world are the same as Christ's. He thinks about people and things just as Christ does. All life becomes to him the raw nectar which the Spirit within him turns into the honey of paradise.

Yet this is not automatic. To do His gracious work God must have the intelligent co-operation of His people. If we would think God's thoughts we must learn to think continually of God. 'God thinks continually of each one of us as if He had no one but ourselves,' said Francois Malaval; 'it is therefore no more than just if we think continuously of Him, as if we had no one but Himself.'

We must think of the surrounding world of people and things against the background of our thoughts of God. The experienced Christian will never think of anything directly; his thoughts go first to God and from God out to His creation. His thoughts, like the angels of Jacob's ladder, ascend and descend, but ever God stands above them presiding over all.

To be heavenly-minded we must think heavenly thoughts. 'So let us return to ourselves, brothers,...for it is impossible for us to be reconciled and united with God if we do not first return to ourselves,...striving constantly to keep attention on the kingdom of heaven which is within us.'

So wrote Nicephorus, a father of the Greek Orthodox

Church, in the fourteenth century, and nothing since has changed. God must have all our thoughts if we would experience the sanctification of our minds.

30

The Futility of Regret

The human heart is heretical by nature. Popular religious beliefs should be checked carefully against the Word of God, for they are almost certain to be wrong.

Legalism, for instance, is natural to the human heart. Grace in its true New Testament meaning is foreign to human reason, not because it is contrary to reason but because it lies beyond it. The doctrine of grace had to be revealed; it could not have been discovered.

The essence of legalism is self-atonement. The seeker tries to make himself acceptable to God by some act of restitution, or by self-punishment or the feeling of regret. The desire to be pleasing to God is commendable certainly, but the effort to please God by self-effort is not, for it assumes that sin once done may be undone, an assumption wholly false.

Long after we have learned from the Scriptures that we cannot by fasting, or the wearing of a hair shirt or the making of many prayers, atone for the sins of the soul, we still tend by a kind of pernicious natural heresy to feel that we can please God and purify our souls by the penance of perpetual regret.

This latter is the Protestant's unacknowledged penance. Though he claims to believe in the doctrine of justification by faith he still secretly feels that what he calls 'godly sorrow' will make him dear to God. Though he may know better he is caught in the web of a wrong religious feeling and betrayed.

There is indeed a godly sorrow that worketh repentance, and it must be acknowledged that among us Christians this feeling is often not present in sufficient strength to work real repentance; but the persistence of this sorrow till it become chronic regret is neither right nor good. Regret is a kind of frustrated repentance that has not been quite consummated. Once the soul has turned from all sin and committed itself wholly to God there is no longer any legitimate place for regret. When moral innocence has been restored by the forgiving love of God the guilt may be remembered, but the sting is gone from the memory. The forgiven man knows that he has sinned, but he no longer feels it.

The effort to be forgiven by works is one that can never be completed because no one knows or can know how much is enough to cancel out the offence; so the seeker must go on year after year paying on his moral debt, here a little, there a little, knowing that he sometimes adds to his bill much more than he pays. The task of keeping books on such a transaction can never end, and the seeker can only hope that when the last entry is made he may be ahead and the account fully paid. This is quite the popular belief, this forgiveness by self-effort, but it is a natural heresy and can at last only betray those who depend upon it.

It may be argued that the absence of regret indicates a low and inadequate view of sin, but the exact opposite is true. Sin is so frightful, so destructive to the soul that no human thought or act can in any degree diminish its lethal effects. Only God can deal with it successfully; only the blood of Christ can cleanse it from the pores of the spirit. The heart that has been delivered from this dread enemy feels not regret but wondrous relief and unceasing gratitude.

The returned prodigal honours his father more by

rejoicing than by repining. Had the young man in the story had less faith in his father he might have mourned in a corner instead of joining in the festivities. His confidence in the loving-kindness of his father gave him the courage to forget his chequered past.

Regret frets the soul as tension frets the nerves and anxiety the mind. I believe that the chronic unhappiness of most Christians may be attributed to a gnawing uneasiness lest God has not fully forgiven them, or the fear that He expects as the price of His forgiveness some sort of emotional penance which they have not furnished. As our confidence in the goodness of God mounts our anxieties will diminish and our moral happiness rise in inverse proportion.

Regret may be no more than a form of self-love. A man may have such a high regard for himself that any failure to live up to his own image of himself disappoints him deeply. He feels that he has betrayed his better self by his act of wrong-doing, and even if God is willing to forgive him he will not forgive himself. Sin brings to such a man a painful loss of face that is not soon forgotten. He becomes permanently angry with himself and tries to punish himself by going to God frequently with petulant self-accusations. This state of mind crystallises finally into a feeling of chronic regret which appears to be a proof of deep penitence but is actually proof of deep self-love.

Regret for a sinful past will remain until we truly believe that for us in Christ that sinful past no longer exists. The man in Christ has only Christ's past and that is perfect and acceptable to God. In Christ he died, in Christ he rose, and in Christ he is seated within the circle of God's favoured ones. He is no longer angry with himself because he is no longer self-regarding, but Christ-regarding; hence there is no place for regret.

31

The Importance of Self-judgement

Hardly anything else reveals so well the fear and uncertainty among men as the length to which they will go to hide their true selves from each other and even from their own eyes.

Almost all men live from childhood to death behind a semi-opaque curtain, coming out briefly only when forced by some emotional shock and then retreating as quickly as possible into hiding again. The result of this lifelong dissimulation is that people rarely know their neighbours for what they really are, and worse than that, the camouflage is so successful that mostly they do not quite know themselves either.

Self-knowledge is so critically important to us in our pursuit of God and His righteousness that we lie under heavy obligation to do immediately whatever is necessary to remove the disguise and permit our real selves to be known. It is one of the supreme tragedies in religion that so many of us think so highly of ourselves when the evidence lies all on the other side; and our self-admiration effectively blocks out any possible effort to discover a remedy for our condition. Only the man who knows he is sick will go to a physician.

Now, our true moral and spiritual state can be disclosed only by the Spirit and the Word. The final judgement of the heart is God's. There is a sense in which we dare not judge each other (Mt 7:1–5), and in which we should not even try to judge ourselves (1 Cor 4:3). The ultimate judgement belongs to the one whose eyes are like a flame of fire and who sees quite through the deeds and thoughts of men. I for one am glad to leave the final word with Him.

There is, nevertheless, a place for self-judgement and a real need that we exercise it (1 Cor 11:31, 32). While our self-discovery is not likely to be complete and our self-judgement is almost certain to be biased and imperfect, there is yet every good reason for us to work along with the Holy Spirit in His benign effort to locate us spiritually in order that we may make such amendments as the circumstances demand. That God already knows us thoroughly is certain (Ps 139:1–6). It remains for us to know ourselves as accurately as possible. For this reason I offer some rules for self-discovery; and if the results are not all we could desire they may be at least better than none at all. We may be known by the following:

1. *What we want most.* We have but to get quiet, recollect our thoughts, wait for the mild excitement within us to subside, and then listen closely for the faint cry of desire. Ask your heart, What would you rather have than anything else in the world? Reject the conventional answer. Insist on the true one, and when you have heard it you will know the kind of person you are.

2. *What we think about most.* The necessities of life compel us to think about many things, but the true test is what we think about *voluntarily*. It is more than likely that our thoughts will cluster about our secret heart treasure, and whatever that is will reveal what we are. 'Where your treasure is, there will your heart be also.'

3. *How we use our money.* Again we must ignore those matters about which we are not altogether free. We must pay taxes and provide the necessities of life for ourselves and family, if any. That is routine, merely, and tells us little about ourselves. But whatever money is left

to do with as we please—that will tell us a great deal indeed. Better listen to it.

4. *What we do with our leisure time.* A large share of our time is already spoken for by the exigencies of civilised living, but we do have some free time. What we do with it is vital. Most people waste it staring at the television, listening to the radio, reading the cheap output of the press or engaging in idle chatter. What I do with mine reveals the kind of man I am.

5. *The company we enjoy.* There is a law of moral attraction that draws every man to the society most like himself. 'Being let go, they went to their own company.' Where we go when we are free to go where we will is a near-infallible index of character.

6. *Whom and what we admire.* I have long suspected that the great majority of evangelical Christians, while kept somewhat in line by the pressure of group opinion, nevertheless have a boundless, if perforce secret, admiration for the world. We can learn the true state of our minds by examining our unexpressed admirations. Israel often admired, even envied, the pagan nations around them, and so forgot the adoption and the glory and the covenants and the law and the promises and the fathers. Instead of blaming Israel let us look to ourselves.

7. *What we laugh at.* No one with a due regard for the wisdom of God would argue that there is anything wrong with laughter, since humour is a legitimate component of our complex nature. Lacking a sense of humour we fall that much short of healthy humanity.

But the test we are running here is not whether we laugh or not, but what we laugh at. Some things lie outside the field of pure humour. No reverent Christian, for instance, finds death funny, nor birth nor love. No Spirit-filled man can bring himself to laugh at the Holy Scriptures, or the Church which Christ purchased with His own blood, or prayer or righteousness or human grief or pain. And surely no one who has been even for a brief moment in the presence of God could ever laugh at a story involving the Deity.

These are a few tests. The wise Christian will find others.

32

Serving in the Emergency

One mighty fact there is which for us men overwhelms all other considerations and gives significance to everything we do. It is that the human race has left its first estate and is morally and spiritually fallen.

Since the fall of man the earth has been a disaster area and everyone lives with a critical emergency. Nothing is normal. Everything is wrong and everyone is wrong until made right by the redeeming work of Christ and the effective operation of the Holy Spirit.

The universal disaster of the fall compels us to think differently about our obligation to our fellow men. What would be entirely permissible under normal conditions becomes wrong in the present situation, and many things not otherwise required are necessary because of abnormal conditions.

It is in view of this that all our Christian service must be evaluated. The needs of the people, not our own convenience, decide how far we shall go and how much we shall do. Had there been no disaster there would have been no need for the Eternal Son to empty Himself and descend to Bethlehem's manger. Had there been no fall there would have been no incarnation, no thorns, no cross. These resulted when the divine goodness confronted the human emergency.

While Christ was the perfect example of the healthy normal man, He yet did not live a normal life. He sacrificed many pure enjoyments to give Himself to the holy work of moral rescue. His conduct was determined not by what was legitimate or innocent, but by our human need. He pleased not Himself but lived for the emergency; and as He was so are we in this world.

Before the judgement seat of Christ my service will be judged not by how much I have done but by how much I could have done. In God's sight my giving is measured not by how much I have given but by how much I could have given and how much I had left after I made my gift. The needs of the world and my total ability to minister to those needs decide the worth of my service.

Not by its size is my gift judged, but by how much of me there is in it. No man gives at all until he has given all. No man gives anything acceptable to God until he has first given himself in love and sacrifice.

The hero is cited by his country not for the number of persons he has saved only, but for the degree of danger to himself present in his act. Service that can be done without peril, that carries no loss, no sacrifice, does not rate high in the sight of men or God.

In the work of the church the amount one man must do to accomplish a given task is determined by how much or how little the rest of the company is willing to do. It is a rare church whose members all put their shoulder to the wheel. The typical church is composed of the few whose shoulders are bruised by their faithful labours and the many who are unwilling to raise a blister in the service of God and their fellow men. There may be a bit of wry humour in all this, but it is quite certain that there will be no laughter when each of us gives account to God of the deeds done in the body.

I think that most Christians would be better pleased if the Lord did not inquire into their personal affairs too closely. They want Him to save them, keep them happy and take them to heaven at last, but not to be too inquisitive about their conduct or service. But He has searched us and known us; He knows our down-sitting and our up-rising and understands our thoughts afar off. There is no place to hide from those eyes that are as a flame of fire and there is no way to escape from the judgement of those feet that are like fine brass. It is the part of wisdom to live with these things in mind.

God is love and His kindness is unbounded, but He has no sympathy with the carnal mind. He remembers that we are dust, indeed, but He refuses to tolerate the doings of the flesh. He has given us His word; He has promised that we would never be tempted above what we were able to bear; He has placed Himself at our disposal in response to believing prayer; He has made available to us the infinite moral power of His Holy Spirit to enable us to do His will here on earth. There is no excuse for our acting like timid weaklings.

Before there can be acceptable service there must be an acceptable life. Before we can know how much we owe we must learn how great is the need. Men are caught in a disaster worse than earthquake or flood, and the redeemed of the Lord are to work for their rescue.

In considering these things we must not go on the defensive. The Lord loves the artless, the candid, the childlike. He cannot work with those who argue or bargain or plead or excuse themselves. He hides His profoundest mysteries from the wise and the prudent and reveals them unto babes. The poor in spirit always receive the kingdom, the meek inherit the earth, the mourner is comforted and the pure in heart see God.

My old friend Tom Haire, the praying plumber, after several months of ministry in the United States, told me one day that he was going back home for a rest. In the thickest of Irish brogues he explained how it was with him. 'I'm preached out,' he said, 'and I am going back to spend three months waiting on God. There are some spiritual matters that I want to get straightened out. *I*

*want to appear before the judgement seat now while I can
do something about it.'*

33

How to Keep from Going Stale

Periods of staleness in the life are not inevitable but they are common. He is a rare Christian who has not experienced times of spiritual dullness when the relish has gone out of his heart and the enjoyment of living has diminished greatly or departed altogether.

Since there is no single cause of this condition there is no one simple remedy for it. Sometimes we are to blame, as for instance when we do a wrong act without immediately seeking forgiveness and cleansing; or when we permit worldly interests to grow up and choke the tender plants of the inner life.

When the cause is known, and particularly when it is as uncomplex as this, the remedy is the old-fashioned one of repentance. But if after careful and candid examination of the life by prayer and the Word no real evil is discovered, we gain nothing by putting the worst construction on things and lying face down in the dust. To say that we have not sinned when we have is to be false to the fact; to insist that we have sinned when we have not is to be false to ourselves. There comes a time when the most spiritual thing we can do is to accept cleansing from all sin as an accomplished fact and stop calling that unclean which God has called clean.

Sometimes our trouble is not moral but physical. As

long as we are in these mortal bodies our spiritual lives will be to some degree affected by our bodies. Here we should notice that there is a difference between our moral bodies and the 'flesh' of Pauline theology. When Paul speaks of the flesh he refers to our fallen human nature, not to our physical bodies, which are temples of the Holy Spirit. Through the power of the Spirit there is deliverance from the propensities of the flesh, but while we live there is no relief from the weaknesses and imperfections of the body.

One often-unsuspected cause of staleness is fatigue. Shakespeare said something to the effect that no man could be a philosopher when he had a toothache, and while it is possible to be a weary saint, it is scarcely possible to be weary and *feel* saintly; and it is our want of feeling that we are considering here. The Christian who gets tired in the work of the Lord and stays tired without relief beyond a reasonable time will go stale. The fact that he grew weary by toiling in the Lord's vineyard will not make his weariness any less real. Our Lord knew this and occasionally took His disciples aside for a rest.

I sometimes think that our custom of holding the important preaching meeting of the week on Sunday evening forces us ministers to preach some of our best sermons to tired hearers and cuts down on the efficiency of our work. We read with some astonishment that men such as John Bunyan often preached as early as five o'clock in the morning. I know times have changed and I do not propose to announce any five o'clock preaching services; but at least our fathers managed to preach to fresh audiences, while we habitually address tired ones. Undoubtedly they had the advantage.

Another reason some of us become jaded is monotony. To do one thing continuously will result in boredom even if what we do is pleasant; and to think about the same things without cessation will also lead to boredom even if we are thinking about the things of the kingdom. Milton suggests that God made night to alternate with day for the purpose of providing us with 'grateful vicissitude', a welcome change for which we should be thankful.

Some of the purest souls have written of the dangers of continuous spiritual exercises uninterrupted by lowlier considerations. Von Hugel speaks of the 'neural cost' of prayer and advises that we should sometimes break off thoughts of heavenly things and go for a walk or dig in the garden. We have all known the disappointment felt when returning to a passage of Scripture that had been so fresh and fragrant the day before only to find the sweetness gone out of it. It is the Spirit's way of urging us on to new vistas. I notice that in the wilderness God kept Israel moving. One may wonder what would have happened if they had camped in one place for forty years.

The lives of the great Christians show that they differed not only from each other but from themselves at different periods of their lives. Spiritual exercises that helped them at one stage of their development later became useless and had to be changed for others.

To stay free from religious ennui we should be careful not to get into a rut, not even a good rut. Our Lord warned against vain repetition. There is repetition that is not vain, but oft-repeated prayers become vain when they have lost their urgency. We should examine our prayers every now and again to discover how much sincerity and spontaneity they possess. We should insist on keeping them simple, candid, fresh and original. And above all we should never seek to induce holy emotions. When we feel dry it is wise either to ignore it or to tell God about it without any sense of guilt. If we are dry because of some wrong on our part the Spirit through the Word will show us the fault.

In short, we can keep from going stale by getting proper rest, by practising complete candour in prayer, by introducing variety into our lives, by heeding God's call to move onward and by exercising quiet faith always.

34

Marks of the Spiritual Man

The concept of spirituality varies among different Christian groups. In some circles the highly vocal person who talks religion continually is thought to be very spiritual; others accept noisy exuberance as a mark of spirituality, and in some churches the man who prays first, longest and loudest gets a reputation for being the most spiritual man in the assembly.

Now a vigorous testimony, frequent prayers and loud praise may be entirely consistent with spirituality, but it is important that we understand that they do not in themselves constitute it nor prove that it is present.

True spirituality manifests itself in certain dominant desires. These are ever-present, deep-settled wants sufficiently powerful to motivate and control the life. For convenience let me number them, though I make no effort to decide the order of their importance.

1. First is the desire to be holy rather than happy. The yearning after happiness found so widely among Christians professing a superior degree of sanctity is sufficient proof that such sanctity is not indeed present. The truly spiritual man knows that God will give abundance of joy after we have become able to receive it without injury to our souls, but he does not demand it at once. John Wesley said of the members of one of the early Method-

ist societies that he doubted that they had been made perfect in love because they came to church to enjoy religion instead of to learn how they could become holy.

2. A man may be considered spiritual when he wants to see the honour of God advanced through his life even if it means that he himself must suffer temporary dishonour or loss. Such a man prays 'Hallowed be Thy name', and silently adds, 'at any cost to me, Lord.' He lives for God's honour by a kind of spiritual reflex. Every choice involving the glory of God is for him already made before it presents itself. He does not need to debate the matter with his own heart; there is nothing to debate. The glory of God is necessary to him; he gasps for it as a suffocating man gasps for air.

3. The spiritual man wants to carry his cross. Many Christians accept adversity or tribulation with a sigh and call it their cross, forgetting that such things come alike to saint and sinner. The cross is that extra adversity that comes to us as a result of our obedience to Christ. This cross is not forced upon us; we voluntarily take it up with full knowledge of the consequences. We choose to obey Christ and by so doing choose to carry the cross.

Carrying a cross means to be attached to the person of Christ, committed to the lordship of Christ and obedient to the commandments of Christ. The man who is so attached, so committed, so obedient is a spiritual man.

4. Again, a Christian is spiritual when he sees everything from God's viewpoint. The ability to weigh all things in the divine scale and place the same value upon them as God does is the mark of a Spirit-filled life.

God looks *at* and *through* at the same time. His gaze does not rest on the surface but penetrates to the true meaning of things. The carnal Christian looks at an object or a situation, but because he does not see through it he is elated or cast down by what he sees. The spiritual man is able to look through things as God looks and think of them as God thinks. He insists on seeing all things as God sees them even if it humbles him and exposes his ignorance to the point of real pain.

5. Another desire of the spiritual man is to die right rather than to live wrong. A sure mark of the mature man of God is his nonchalance about living. The earth-loving, body-conscious Christian looks upon death with numb terror in his heart; but as he goes on to live in the Spirit he becomes increasingly indifferent to the number of his years here below, and at the same time increasingly careful of the kind of life he lives while he is here. He will not purchase a few extra days of life at the cost of compromise or failure. He wants most of all to be right, and he is happy to let God decide how long he shall live. He knows that he can afford to die now that he is in Christ, but he knows that he cannot afford to do wrong, and this knowledge becomes a gyroscope to stabilise his thinking and his acting.

6. The desire to see others advance at his expense is another mark of the spiritual man. He wants to see other Christians above him and is happy when they are promoted and he is overlooked. There is no envy in his heart; when his brethren are honoured he is pleased because such is the will of God and that will is his earthly heaven. If God is pleased, he is pleased for that reason, and if it pleases God to exalt another above him he is content to have it so.

7. The spiritual man habitually makes eternity-judgements instead of time-judgements. By faith he rises above the tug of earth and the flow of time and learns to think and feel as one who has already left the world and gone to join the innumerable company of angels and the general assembly and church of the First-born which are written in heaven. Such a man would rather be useful than famous and would rather serve than be served.

And all this must be by the operation of the Holy Spirit within him. No man can become spiritual by himself. Only the free Spirit can make a man spiritual.

35

Chastisement and Cross-carrying Not the Same

For the Christian cross-carrying and chastisement are alike but not identical. They differ in a number of important ways. The two ideas are usually considered to be the same and the words embodying the ideas are used interchangeably. There is, however, a sharp distinction between them. When we confuse them we are not thinking accurately; and when we do not think accurately about truth we lose some benefit that we might otherwise enjoy.

The cross and the rod occur close together in the Holy Scriptures, but they are not the same thing. The rod is imposed without the consent of the one who suffers it. The cross cannot be imposed by another. Even Christ bore the cross by His own free choice. He said of the life He poured out on the cross, 'No man taketh it from me, but I lay it down of myself.' He had every opportunity to escape the cross but He set His face like a flint to go to Jerusalem to die. The only compulsion He knew was the compulsion of love.

Chastisement is an act of God; cross-carrying an act of the Christian. When God in love lays the rod to the back of His children He does not ask permission. Chastisement for the believer is not voluntary except in the sense that he chooses the will of God with the knowledge that the will of God includes chastisement. 'For whom the Lord loveth he chasteneth, and scourgeth every son whom he receiveth. If ye endure chastening, God dealeth with you as with sons; for what son is he whom the father chasteneth not?'

The cross never comes unsolicited; the rod always does. 'If any man will come after me, let him deny himself, and take up his cross, and follow me.' Here is clear, intelligent choice, a choice that must be made by the individual with determination and forethought. In the kingdom of God no one ever stumbled onto a cross.

But what is the cross for the Christian? Obviously it is not the wooden instrument the Romans used to execute the sentence of death upon persons guilty of capital crimes. The cross is the suffering the Christian endures as a consequence of his following Christ in perfect obedience. Christ chose the cross by choosing the path that led to it; and it is so with His followers. In the way of obedience stands the cross, and we take the cross when we enter that way.

As the cross stands in the way of obedience, so chastisement is found in the way of disobedience. God never chastens a perfectly obedient child. Consider the fathers of our flesh; they never punished us for obedience, only for disobedience.

When we feel the sting of the rod we may be sure we are temporarily out of the right way. Conversely, the pain of the cross means that we are in the way. But the Father's love is not more or less, wherever we may be. God chastens us not that He may love us but because He loves us. In a well-ordered house a disobedient child may expect punishment; in the household of God no careless Christian can hope to escape it.

But how can we tell in a given situation whether our pain is from the cross or the rod? Pain is pain from whatever source it comes. Jonah in flight from the will of God suffered no worse storm than did Paul in the centre of God's will; the same wild sea threatened the life of both. And Daniel in the lion's den was in trouble as deep as was Jonah in the whale's belly. The nails bit as deep into the hands of Christ dying for the sins of the world as into the hands of the two thieves dying for their own sins. How then may we distinguish the cross from the rod?

I think the answer is plain. When tribulation comes we have but to note whether it is imposed or chosen. 'Blessed are ye,' said our Lord, 'when men shall revile you, and persecute you, and shall say all manner of evil against you...' But that is not all. Four other words He added: they are '...falsely, for my sake' (Matt 5:11). These words show that the suffering must come voluntarily, that it must be chosen in the larger choice of Christ and righteousness. If the accusation men cry against us is true, no blessedness follows.

We delude ourselves when we try to turn our just punishments into a cross and rejoice over that for which we should rather repent. 'For what glory is it, if, when ye be buffeted for your faults, ye shall take it patiently? but if, when ye do well, and suffer for it, ye take it patiently, this is acceptable with God' (1 Pet 2:20). The cross is always in the way of righteousness. We feel the pain of the cross only when we suffer for Christ's sake by our own willing choice.

I think that there is also another kind of suffering, one that does not fall into either of the categories considered above. It comes neither from the rod nor from the cross, not being imposed as a moral corrective nor suffered as a result of our Christian life and testimony. It comes in the course of nature and arises from the many ills flesh is heir to. It visits all alike in a greater or lesser degree and would appear to have no clear spiritual significance. Its source may be fire, flood, bereavement, injuries, accidents, illness, old age, weariness or the upset conditions of the world generally. What are we to do about this?

Well, some great souls have managed to turn even these neutral afflictions to good. By prayer and self-abasement they wooed adversity to become their friend and made rough distress a teacher to instruct them in the heavenly arts. May we not emulate them?

36

The Wind in Our Face

'God hath called you to Christ's side,' wrote the saintly Rutherford, 'and the wind is now in Christ's face in this land; and seeing ye are with Him, ye cannot expect the leeside or the sunny side of the brae.'

With that beautiful feeling for words that characterised Samuel Rutherford's most casual utterance he here crystallises for us one of the great radical facts of the Christian life. The wind is in Christ's face, and because we go with Him we too shall have the wind in our face. We should not expect less.

The yearning for the sunny side of the brae is natural enough, and for such sensitive creatures as we are it is, I suppose, quite excusable. No one enjoys walking into a cold wind. Yet the church has had to march with the wind in her face through the long centuries.

In our eagerness to make converts I am afraid we have lately been guilty of using the technique of modern salesmanship, which is of course to present only the desirable qualities in a product and ignore the rest. We go to men and offer them a cosy home on the sunny side of the brae. If they will but accept Christ He will give them peace of mind, solve their problems, prosper their business, protect their families and keep them happy all day long. They believe us and come, and the first cold wind sends them shivering to some counsellor to find out what has gone wrong; and that is the last we hear of many of them.

The teachings of Christ reveal Him to be a realist in the finest meaning of that word. Nowhere in the Gospels do we find anything visionary or over-optimistic. He told His hearers the whole truth and let them make up their minds. He might grieve over the retreating form of an inquirer who could not face up to the truth, but He never ran after him to try to win him with rosy promises. He would have men follow Him, knowing the cost, or He would let them go their ways.

All this is but to say that Christ is honest. We can trust Him. He knows that He will never be popular among the sons of Adam and He knows that His followers need not expect to be. The wind that blows in His face will be felt by all who travel with Him, and we are not intellectually honest when we try to hide that fact from them.

By offering our hearers a sweetness-and-light gospel and promising every taker a place on the sunny side of the brae, we not only cruelly deceive them, we guarantee also a high casualty rate among the converts won on such terms. On certain foreign fields the expression 'rice Christians' has been coined to describe those who adopt Christianity for profit. The experienced missionary knows that the convert that must pay a heavy price for his faith in Christ is the one that will persevere to the end. He begins with the wind in his face, and should the storm grow in strength he will not turn back for he has been conditioned to endure it.

By playing down the cost of discipleship we are producing rice Christians by the tens of thousands right here on the North American continent. Old-timers will remember the Florida land boom of some years ago when a few unscrupulous real estate brokers got rich by selling big chunks of alligator swamp to innocent Northerners at fancy prices. Right now there's a boom in religious real estate on the sunny side of the brae. Thousands are investing and a few promoters are getting rich; but when the public finds out what it has bought some of those same promoters are going out of business. And it can't happen too soon.

What has Christ to offer to us that is sound, genuine and desirable? He offers forgiveness of sins, inward cleansing, peace with God, eternal life, the gift of the Holy Spirit, victory over temptation, resurrection from the dead, a glorified body, immortality and a dwelling place in the house of the Lord for ever. These are a few benefits that come to us as a result of faith in Christ and total committal to Him. Add to these the expanding wonders and increasing glories that shall be ours through the long, long reaches of eternity, and we get an imperfect idea of what Paul called 'the unsearchable riches of Christ'.

To accept the call of Christ changes the returning sinner indeed, but it does not change the world. The wind still blows toward hell and the man who is walking in the opposite direction will have the wind in his face. And we had better take this into account when we ponder on spiritual things. If the unsearchable riches of Christ are not worth suffering for, then we should know it now and cease to play at religion.

When the rich young ruler learned the cost of discipleship he went away sorrowing. He could not give up the sunny side of the brae. But thanks be to God, there are some in every age who refuse to go back. The Acts of the Apostles is the story of men and women who turned their faces into the stiff wind of persecution and loss and followed the Lamb whithersoever He went. They knew that the world hated Christ without a cause and hated them for His sake; but for the glory that was set before them they continued steadfastly on the way.

Perhaps the whole thing can be reduced to a simple matter of faith or unbelief. Faith sees afar the triumph of Christ and is willing to endure any hardship to share in it. Unbelief is not sure of anything except that it hates the wind and loves the sunny side of the brae. Every man will have to decide for himself whether or not he can afford the terrible luxury of unbelief.

37

The Friends of God

The idea of the divine–human friendship originated with
God. Had not God said first 'Ye are my friends' it would
be inexcusably brash for any man to say 'I am a friend of
God.' But since He claims us for His friends it is an act of
unbelief to ignore or deny the relationship.

As with every other relationship affecting moral intel-
ligences, our friendship with God is capable of degrees,
grading up from the formal to the intimate. We all know
persons whom we properly call friends but whose friendship is so fragile and tenuous as to stand almost no strain
without breaking. And there are friends, usually only a
few, whose friendship has been tried in the fire of long
experience and which it would be next to impossible to
destroy.

Even though radically different from each other, two
persons may enjoy the closest friendship for a lifetime;
for it is not a requisite of friendship that the participants
be alike in all things; it is enough that they be alike at the
points where their personalities touch. Harmony is likeness at points of contact, and friendship is likeness where
hearts merge.

For this reason the whole idea of the divine–human
friendship is logical enough and entirely credible. The
infinite God and the finite man can merge their person-

alities in the tenderest, most satisfying friendship. In such a relationship there is no idea of equality; only of likeness where the heart of man meets the heart of God.

This likeness is possible because God at the first made man in His own image and because He is now re-making men in the image that was lost by sin.

The image of God in man cannot extend to every part of man's being, for God has attributes which He cannot impart to any of His creatures, however favoured. God is uncreated, self-existent, infinite, sovereign, eternal; these attributes are His alone and by their very definition cannot be shared with another. But there are other attributes which He can impart to His creatures and in some measure share with His redeemed children.

Intellect, self-consciousness, love, goodness, holiness, pity, faithfulness—these and certain other attributes are the points where likeness between God and man may be achieved. It is here that the divine—human friendship is experienced.

God, being perfect, has capacity for perfect friendship. Man, being imperfect, can never quite know perfection in anything, least of all in his relation to the incomprehensible Godhead. Perfection lies on God's side, but on man's side there are weakness of purpose, lack of desire, small faith and numerous other impediments. These make for a friendship which, though it is the most wonder-filled experience possible to man, is yet short of that completeness we would enjoy if these impediments were removed or even reduced appreciably.

Though the truth compels us to admit these imperfections on our side of the divine—human friendship, yet there is no reason to despair. In spite of our human frailties we can grow in grace and move progressively toward a more perfect experiential union with God. This we can do by firm self-discipline, quick obedience, unceasing prayer, utter detachment from the world and the exercise of robust faith in the truths revealed in the Holy Scriptures.

It should be pointed out that no revealed truth becomes automatically effective. The effect any truth has upon us depends upon our attitude toward it. First it must be accepted in active faith and received into our minds as completely trustworthy and beyond dispute. It must become a kind of dye to give colour to all of our thinking and praying.

The more perfect our friendship with God becomes the simpler will our lives be. Those formalities that are so necessary to keep a casual friendship alive may be dispensed with when true friends sit in each other's presence. True friends trust each other.

There is a great difference between having 'company' and having a friend in the house. The friend we can treat as a member of the family, but company must be entertained.

God is not satisfied until there exists between Him and His people a relaxed informality that requires no artificial stimulation. The true friend of God may sit in His presence for long periods in silence. Complete trust needs no words of assurance. Such words have long ago been spoken and the adoring heart can safely be still before God.

Unquestionably the highest privilege granted to man on earth is to be admitted into the circle of the friends of God. Nothing is important enough to be allowed to stand in the way of our relation to God.

Nothing in heaven or earth or hell can separate us from the love of God; we should see to it that nothing on earth shall separate us from God's friendship.

38

The Ministry of the Night

If God has singled you out to be a special object of His grace you may expect Him to honour you with stricter discipline and greater suffering than less favoured ones are called upon to endure.

And right here let me anticipate the objection someone is sure to raise, viz., that God has no 'specials' among His children. The Holy Scriptures and Christian history agree to show that He has. Star differs from star in glory among the saints on earth as well as among the glorified in heaven. Without question the differences exist; but whether they are by the decree of God or by His foreknowledge of the degree of receptivity He will find among His children I am not prepared to say with certainty, though I would lean strongly to the latter view.

If God sets out to make you an unusual Christian He is not likely to be as gentle as He is usually pictured by the popular teachers. A sculptor does not use a manicure set to reduce the rude, unshapely marble to a thing of beauty. The saw, the hammer and the chisel are cruel tools, but without them the rough stone must remain for ever formless and unbeautiful.

To do His supreme work of grace within you He will take from your heart everything you love most. Everything you trust in will go from you. Piles of ashes will lie where your most precious treasures used to be.

This is not to teach the sanctifying power of poverty. If to be poor made men holy every tramp on a park bench would be a saint. But God knows the secret of removing things from our hearts while they still remain to us. What He does is to restrain us from enjoying them. He lets us have them but makes us psychologically unable to let our hearts go out to them. Thus they are useful without being harmful.

All this God will accomplish at the expense of the common pleasures that have up to that time supported your life and made it zestful. Now under the careful treatment of the Holy Spirit your life may become dry, tasteless and to some degree a burden to you.

While in this state you will exist by a kind of blind will to live; you will find none of the inward sweetness you had enjoyed before. The smile of God will be for the time withdrawn, or at least hidden from your eyes. Then you will learn what faith is; you will find out the hard way, but the only way open to you, that true faith lies in the will, that the joy unspeakable of which the apostle speaks is not itself faith but a slow-ripening fruit of faith; and you will learn that present spiritual joys may come and go as they will without altering your spiritual status or in any way affecting your position as a true child of the Heavenly Father. And you will also learn, probably to your astonishment, that it is possible to live in all good conscience before God and men and still feel nothing of the 'peace and joy' you hear talked about so much by immature Christians.

How long you continue in this night of the soul will depend upon a number of factors, some of which you may be able later to identify; while others will remain with God, completely hidden from you. The words 'The day is thine, the night also is thine' will now be interpreted for you by the best of all teachers, the Holy Spirit;

and you will know by personal experience what a blessed thing is the ministry of the night.

But there is a limit to man's ability to live without joy. Even Christ could endure the cross only because of the joy set before Him. The strongest steel breaks if kept too long under unrelieved tension. God knows exactly how much pressure each one of us can take. He knows how long we can endure the night, so He gives the soul relief, first by welcome glimpses of the morning star and then by the fuller light that harbingers the morning.

Slowly you will discover God's love in your suffering. Your heart will begin to approve the whole thing. You will learn from yourself what all the schools in the world could not teach you—the healing action of faith without supporting pleasure. You will feel and understand the ministry of the night; its power to purify, to detach, to humble, to destroy the fear of death and, what is more important to you at the moment, the fear of life. And you will learn that sometimes pain can do what even joy cannot, such as exposing the vanity of earth's trifles and filling your heart with longing for the peace of heaven.

What I write here is in no way original. This has been discovered anew by each generation of Christian seekers and is almost a cliché of the deeper life. Yet it needs to be said to this generation of believers often and with emphasis, for the type of Christianity now in vogue does not include anything as serious and as difficult as this. The quest of the modern Christian is likely to be for peace of mind and spiritual joy, with a good degree of material prosperity thrown in as an external proof of the divine favour.

Some will understand this, however, even if the number is relatively small, and they will constitute the hard core of practising saints so badly needed at this serious hour if New Testament Christianity is to survive to the next generation.

39

The Art of True Worship*

Philosophers have noted the vast difference between men and beasts and have tried to find that difference in one or another distinguishing characteristic. They have said, for instance, that man is the thinking animal, or that he is the laughing animal, or that he is the only animal with a conscience. The one mark, however, which for ever distinguishes man from all other forms of life on earth is that he is a worshipper; he has a bent toward and a capacity for worship.

Apart from his position as a worshipper of God, man has no sure key to his own being; he is but a higher animal, being born much as any other animal, going through the cycle of his life here on earth and dying at last without knowing what the whole thing is about. If that is all for him, if he has no more reason than the beast for living, then it is an odd thing indeed that he is the only one of the animals that worries about himself, that wonders, that asks questions of the universe. The very fact that he does these things tells the wise man that somewhere there is one to whom he owes allegiance, one before whom he should kneel and do homage.

*Reprinted by permission from *Moody Monthly*. Copyright Moody Bible Institute, 1952.

The Christian revelation tells us that that one is God the Father Almighty, maker of heaven and earth, who is to be worshipped in the Spirit in the name of Jesus Christ our Lord. That is enough for us. Without trying to reason it out we may proceed from there. All our doubts we meet with faith's wondering affirmation: 'O Lord God, thou knowest,' an utterance which Samuel Taylor Coleridge declared to be the profoundest in human speech.

In worship several elements may be distinguished, among them love, admiration, wonder and adoration. Though they may not be experienced in that order, a little thought will reveal those elements as being present wherever true worship is found.

Both the Old and the New Testament teach that the essence of true worship is the love of God. 'Thou shalt love the Lord thy God with all thy heart, and with all thy soul, and with all thy might.' Our Lord declared this to be the sum of the Law and the Prophets.

Now, love is both a principle and an emotion; it is something both felt and willed. It is capable of almost infinite degrees. Love in the human heart may begin so modestly as to be hardly perceptible and go on to become a raging torrent that sweeps its possessor before it in total helplessness. Something like this must have been the experience of the apostle Paul, for he felt it necessary to explain to his critics that his apparent madness was actually the love of God ravishing his willing heart.

It is quite impossible to worship God without loving Him. Scripture and reason agree to declare this. And God is never satisfied with anything less than *all:* 'all thy heart...all thy soul...all thy might.' This may not at first be possible, but deeper experience with God will prepare us for it, and the inward operations of the Holy

Spirit will enable us after a while to offer Him such a poured-out fullness of love.

In the love which any intelligent creature feels for God there must always be a measure of mystery. It is even possible that it is almost wholly mystery, and that our attempt to find reasons is merely a rationalising of a love already mysteriously present in the heart as a result of some secret operation of the Spirit within us, working like a miner, toiling unseen in the depths of the earth. But so far as reasons can be given, they would seem to be two: gratitude and excellence. To love God because He has been good to us is one of the most reasonable things possible. The love which arises from the consideration of His kindness to us is valid and altogether acceptable to Him. It is nevertheless a lower degree of love, being less selfless than that love which springs from an appreciation of what God is in Himself apart from His gifts.

Thus the simple love which arises from gratitude, when expressed in any act or conscious utterance, is undoubtedly worship. But the quality of our worship is stepped up as we move away from the thought of what God has done for us and nearer the thought of the excellence of His holy nature. This leads us to admiration.

The dictionary says that to admire is 'to regard with wondering esteem accompanied by pleasure and delight; to look at or upon with an elevated feeling of pleasure'. According to this definition, God has few admirers among Christians today.

Many are they who are grateful for His goodness in providing salvation. At Thanksgiving time the churches ring with songs of gratitude that 'all is safely gathered in'. Testimony meetings are mostly devoted to recitations of incidents where someone got into trouble and got out again in answer to prayer. To decry this would be uncharitable and unscriptural, for there is much of the same thing in the Book of Psalms. It is good and right to render unto God thanksgiving for all His mercies to us. But God's admirers, where are they?

The simple truth is that worship is elementary until it begins to take on the quality of admiration. Just as long as the worshipper is engrossed with himself and his good fortune, he is a babe. We begin to grow up when our worship passes from thanksgiving to admiration. As our hearts rise to God in lofty esteem for that which He is ('I AM THAT I AM'), we begin to share a little of the selfless pleasure which is the portion of the blessed in heaven.

The third stage of true worship is wonder. Here the mind ceases to understand and goes over to a kind of delightful astonishment. Carlyle said that worship is 'transcendent wonder', a degree of wonder without limit and beyond expression. That kind of worship is found throughout the Bible (though it is only fair to say that the lesser degrees of worship are found there also). Abraham fell on his face in holy wonderment as God spoke to him. Moses hid his face before the presence of God in the burning bush. Paul could hardly tell whether he was in or out of the body when he was allowed to see the unspeakable glories of the third heaven. When John saw Jesus walking among His churches, he fell at His feet as dead. We cite these as a few examples; the list is long in the biblical record.

It may be said that such experiences as these are highly unusual and can be no criterion for the plain Christian today. This is true, but only of the external circumstances; the spiritual content of the experiences is unchanging and is found alike wherever true believers are found. It is always true that an encounter with God brings wonderment and awe.

The pages of Christian biography are sweet with the testimonies of enraptured worshippers who met God in intimate experience and could find no words to express all they felt and saw and heard. Christian hymnody takes us where the efforts of common prose break down, and brings the wings of poetic feeling to the aid of the wondering saint. Open an old hymnal and turn to the sections on worship and the divine perfections and you will see the part that wonder has played in worship through the centuries.

But wonder is not yet the last nor highest element in worship. The soaring saint has one more mountain peak to clear before he has reached the rarefied air of purest worship. He must adore.

Neither the word *adoration* nor any of its forms is found in our familiar King James Bible, but the idea is there in full bloom. The great Bible saints were, above all, enraptured lovers of God. The psalms celebrate the love which David (and a few others) felt for the person of God.

As suggested above, Paul admitted that the love of God was in his breast a kind of madness: 'For whether we be beside ourselves, it is of God: or whether we be sober, it is for your cause. For the love of Christ constraineth us.' In Weymouth's translation the passage reads, 'For the love of Christ overmasters us.' The idea appears to be that Paul's love for Christ carried him beyond himself and made him do extravagant things which to a mind untouched with the delights of such love might seem quite irrational.

Perhaps the most serious charge that can be brought against modern Christians is that we are not sufficiently in love with Christ. The Christ of fundamentalism is strong but hardly beautiful. It is rarely that we find anyone aglow with personal love for Christ. I trust it is not uncharitable to say that in my opinion a great deal of praise in conservative circles is perfunctory and forced, where it is not downright insincere.

Many of our popular songs and choruses in praise of Christ are hollow and unconvincing. Some are even shocking in their amorous endearments, and strike a reverent soul as being a kind of flattery offered to one with whom neither composer nor singer is acquainted. The whole thing is in the mood of the love ditty, the only difference being the substitution of the name of Christ for that of the earthly lover.

How different and how utterly wonderful are the emotions aroused by a true and Spirit-incited love for Christ. Such a love may rise to a degree of adoration almost beyond the power of the heart to endure, yet at the same time it will be serious, elevated, chaste and reverent.

Christ can never be known without a sense of awe and fear accompanying the knowledge. He is the fairest among ten thousand, but He is also the Lord high and mighty. He is the friend of sinners, but He is also the terror of devils. He is meek and lowly in heart, but He is also Lord and Christ who will surely come to be the judge of all men. No one who knows Him intimately can ever be flippant in His presence.

The love of Christ both wounds and heals, it fascinates and frightens, it kills and makes alive, it draws and repulses, it sobers and enraptures. There can be nothing more terrible or more wonderful than to be stricken with love for Christ so deeply that the whole being goes out in a pained adoration of His person, an adoration that disturbs and disconcerts while it purges and satisfies and relaxes the deep inner heart.

This love as a kind of moral fragrance is ever detected upon the garments of the saints. In the writings of

Augustine, Bishop of Hippo, for instance, this fragrance is so strong as to be very nearly intoxicating. There are passages in his *Confessions* so passionately sweet as to be unbearable, yet so respectful and self-effacing as to excite pity for the man who thus kneels in adoring wonder, caught between holy love and an equally holy fear.

The list of fragrant saints is long. It includes men and women of every shade of theological thought within the bounds of the orthodox Christian faith. It embraces persons of every social level, every degree of education, every race and colour. This radiant love for Christ is to my mind the true test of catholicity, the one sure proof of membership in the church universal.

It remains only to be said that worship as we have described it here is almost (though, thank God, not quite) a forgotten art in our day. For whatever we can say of modern Bible-believing Christians, it can hardly be denied that we are not remarkable for our spirit of worship. The gospel as preached by good men in our times may save souls, but it does not create worshippers.

Our meetings are characterised by cordiality, humour, affability, zeal and high animal spirits; but hardly anywhere do we find gatherings marked by the overshadowing presence of God. We manage to get along on correct doctrine, fast tunes, pleasing personalities and religious amusements.

How few, how pitifully few are the enraptured souls who languish for love of Christ. The sweet 'madness' that visited such men as Bernard and St. Francis and Richard Rolle and Jonathan Edwards and Samuel Rutherford is scarcely known today. The passionate adorations of Teresa and Madame Guyon are a thing of the past. Christianity has fallen into the hands of leaders who knew not Joseph. The very memory of better days is slowly passing from us and a new type of religious person is emerging. How is the gold tarnished and the silver become lead!

If Bible Christianity is to survive the present world upheaval, we shall need to recapture the spirit of worship. We shall need to have a fresh revelation of the greatness of God and the beauty of Jesus. We shall need to put away our phobias and our prejudices against the deeper life and seek again to be filled with the Holy Spirit. He alone can raise our cold hearts to rapture and restore again the art of true worship.

40

Love's Final Test

A century ago a hymn was often sung in the churches, the first stanza of which ran like this:

> *'Tis a point I long to know,*
> *Oft it causes anxious thought,*
> *Do I love the Lord, or no?*
> *Am I His, or am I not?*

Those who thus confessed their spiritual anxiety were serious-minded, honest men and women who could open their hearts to each other in this manner without self-consciousness or loss of face.

It is an evidence of the essential frivolity of the modern religious mind that this hymn is never sung today, and if mentioned from the pulpit at all it is quoted humorously as an example of old-fashioned religious melodrama and a proof that those who once sang it were not up on the doctrine of grace. Why ask, 'Do I love the Lord, or no?' when any number of personal workers stand by to quote convenient texts from the New Testament to prove that we do?

But we had better not be too cocksure. The gravest question any of us face is whether we do or do not love the Lord. Too much hinges on the answer to pass the matter off lightly. And it is a question that no one can answer for another. Not even the Bible can tell the individual man that he loves the Lord; it can only tell him how he can know whether or not he does. It can and does tell us how to test our hearts for love as a man might test ore for the presence of uranium, but we must do the testing.

Our Lord told His disciples that love and obedience were organically united, that the keeping of His sayings would prove that we loved Him and the failure or refusal to keep them would prove that we did not. This is the true test of love, and we will be wise to face up to it.

The commandments of Christ occupy in the New Testament a place of importance that they do not have in current evangelical thought. The idea that our relation to Christ is revealed by our attitude to His commandments is now considered legalistic by many influential Bible teachers, and the plain words of our Lord are rejected outright or interpreted in a manner to make them conform to religious theories ostensibly based upon the epistles of Paul. Thus the Word of God is denied as boldly by evangelicals as by admitted modernists.

If we lived in a spiritual Utopia where every wind blew toward heaven and every man was a friend of God we Christians could take everything for granted, counting on the new life within us to cause us to do the will of God without effort and more or less unconsciously. Unfortunately we have opposing us the lusts of the flesh, the attractions of the world and the temptations of the devil. These complicate our lives and require us often to make determined moral decisions on the side of Christ and His commandments.

It is the crisis that forces us to take a stand for or against. The patriot may be loyal to his country for half a lifetime without giving much thought to it, but let an unfriendly power solicit him to turn traitor and he will quickly spurn its overtures. His patriotism will be brought out into the open for everyone to see.

So it is in the Christian life. When the 'south wind

blew softly' the ship that carried Paul sailed smoothly enough and no one on board knew who Paul was or how much strength of character lay hidden behind that rather plain exterior. But when the mighty tempest, Euroclydon, burst upon them Paul's greatness was soon the talk of everyone on the ship. The apostle, though himself a prisoner, quite literally took command of the vessel, made decisions and issued orders that meant life or death to the people. And I think the crisis brought to a head something in Paul that had not previously been clear even to him. Beautiful theory was quickly crystallised into hard fact when the tempest struck.

The Christian cannot be certain of the reality and depth of his love until he comes face to face with the commandments of Christ and is forced to decide what to do about them. Then he will know. 'He that loveth me not keepeth not my sayings,' said our Lord. 'He that hath my commandments, and keepeth them, he it is that loveth me.'

So the final test of love is obedience. Not sweet emotions, not willingness to sacrifice, not zeal, but obedience to the commandments of Christ. Our Lord drew a line plain and tight for everyone to see. On one side He placed those who keep His commandments and said, 'These love Me.' On the other side He put those who keep not His sayings, and said, 'These love Me not.'

Love for Christ is a love of willing as well as a love of feeling, and it is psychologically impossible to love Him adequately unless we will to obey His words.

In seeking to learn whether we truly love our Lord we must be careful to apply His own test. False tests can only lead to false conclusions as false signs on the highway lead to wrong destinations. The Lord made it plain enough, but with our genius for getting mixed up we have lost sight of the markers.

I think if we would turn for a while from finespun theological speculations about grace and faith and humbly read the New Testament with a mind to obey what we see there, we would easily find ourselves and know for certain the answer to the question that troubled our fathers and should trouble us: Do we love the Lord or no?

41

Meditating on God

Among Christians of all ages and of varying shades of doctrinal emphasis there has been fairly full agreement on one thing: They all believed that it was important that the Christian with serious spiritual aspirations should learn to meditate long and often on God.

Let a Christian insist upon rising above the poor average of current religious experience and he will soon come up against the need to know God Himself as the ultimate goal of all Christian doctrine. Let him seek to explore the sacred wonders of the Triune Godhead and he will discover that sustained and intelligently directed meditation on the person of God is imperative. To know God well he must think on Him unceasingly. Nothing that man has discovered about himself or God has revealed any short cut to pure spirituality. It is still free, but tremendously costly.

Of course this presupposes at least a fair amount of sound theological knowledge. To seek God apart from His own self-disclosure in the inspired Scriptures is not only futile but dangerous. There must be also a knowledge of and complete trust in Jesus Christ as Lord and Redeemer. Christ is not one of many ways to approach God, nor is He the best of several ways; He is the only way. 'I am the way, the truth, and the life: no man cometh unto the Father, but by me' (Jn 14:6). To believe otherwise is to be something less than a Christian.

I am convinced that the dearth of great saints in these times even among those who truly believe in Christ is due at least in part to our unwillingness to give sufficient time to the cultivation of the knowledge of God. We of the nervous West are victims of the philosophy of activism tragically misunderstood. Getting and spending, going and returning, organising and promoting, buying and selling, working and playing–this alone constitutes living. If we are not making plans or working to carry out plans already made we feel that we are failures, that we are sterile, unfruitful eunuchs, parasites on the body of society. The gospel of work, as someone has called it, has crowded out the gospel of Christ in many Christian churches.

In an effort to get the work of the Lord done we often lose contact with the Lord of the work and quite literally wear our people out as well. I have heard more than one pastor boast that his church was a 'live' one, pointing to the printed calendar as a proof–something on every night and several meetings during the day. Of course this proves nothing except that the pastor and the church are being guided by a bad spiritual philosophy. A great many of these time-consuming activities are useless and others plain ridiculous. 'But,' say the eager beavers who run the religious squirrel cages, 'they provide fellowship and they hold our people together.'

To this I reply that what they provide is not fellowship at all, and if that is the best thing the church has to offer to hold the people together it is not a Christian church in the New Testament meaning of that word. The centre of attraction in a true church is the Lord Jesus Christ. As for fellowship, let the Holy Spirit define it for us: 'And they continued stedfastly in the apostles' doctrine and fellowship, and in breaking of bread, and in prayers' (Acts 2:42).

The worldly man can never rest. He must have 'somewhere to go' and 'something to do'. This is a result of the fall, a symptom of a deep-lying disease, yet a blind religious leadership caters to this terrible restlessness instead of trying to cure it by the Word and the Spirit.

If the many activities engaged in by the average church led to the salvation of sinners or the perfecting of believers they would justify themselves easily and triumphantly; but they do not. My observations have led me to the belief that many, perhaps most, of the activities engaged in by the average church do not contribute in any way to the accomplishing of the true work of Christ on earth. I hope I am wrong, but I am afraid I am right.

Our religious activities should be ordered in such a way as to leave plenty of time for the cultivation of the fruits of solitude and silence. It should be remembered, however, that it is possible to waste such quiet periods as we may be able to snatch for ourselves out of the clamorous day. Our meditation must be directed toward God; otherwise we may spend our time of retiral in quiet converse with ourselves. This may quiet our nerves but will not further our spiritual life in any way.

In coming to God we should place ourselves in His presence with the confidence that He is the aggressor, not we. He has been waiting to manifest Himself to us till such time as our noise and activity have subsided enough for Him to make Himself heard and felt by us. Then we should focus our soul's powers of attention upon the Triune Godhead. Whether one person or another claims our present interest is not important. We can trust the Spirit to bring before our minds the person that we at the moment need most to behold.

One thing more. Do not try to imagine God, or you will have an imaginary God; and certainly do not, as some have done, 'set a chair for Him'. God is Spirit. He dwells in your heart, not your house. Brood on the Scriptures and let faith show you God as He is revealed there. Nothing else can equal this glorious sight.

The Knowledge of the Holy

by A. W. Tozer

'The church has surrendered her once lofty concept of God and has substituted for it one so low, so ignoble, as to be utterly unworthy of thinking, worshipping men. With our loss of a sense of majesty has come the further loss of religious awe and sense of the divine presence. We have lost our spirit of worship and our ability to withdraw inwardly to meet God in adoring silence.'

(from the Author's Introduction)

Dr Tozer encourages us to understand the character of God and rediscover His majesty in a way that will deeply affect our day-to-day living.

A. W. Tozer

 OM Publishing